Kayak Fishing

The Complete Guide

Cory Routh
Foreword by Beau Beasley

Photo by Eric Evans.

Kayak Fishing
The Complete Guide

ISBN-10: 1-892469-19-7
ISBN-13: 978-1-892469-19-9

Published by:
No Nonsense Fly Fishing Guidebooks
P.O. Box 91858
Tucson, AZ 85752-1858
(520) 547-2462
www.nononsenseguides.com

1 2 3 4 5 6 7   12 11 10 09 08
Printed in China.

Editor: Howard W. Fisher
Photographs: by Cory Routh
(except where noted)
Design & Production: Doug Goewey

About the Cover

Front: Kevin Kennedy exploring Lake Smith in Virginia Beach, VA.

Back: Ruthless Fishing Inc. guide Mark Lozier with a nice slot-sized redfish.

The New Sport of Kayak Fishing

It is not often that a radical new approach to fishing comes along. Today's kayak manufacturers have turned to building new models specifically for the fisherman. Fishing kayaks are designed for the angler and provide a new method of covering the water, with distinct advantages.

Kayaks can access shallow waters easier than boats or float tubes, often enabling one to get over a sand or gravel bar and into an area that is seldom fished. Kayaks are quiet and provide a stealthy approach without spooking fish.

Whether you prefer spin, bait, or fly-fishing techniques, a kayak can allow you to explore new waters, or your own home waters, in a new way.

In these pages you will learn about choosing a kayak, proper techniques, and gear. Plus, we have provided a guide to some of the author's favorite waters. If these waters are not in your area, you can still learn the techniques used and apply them to your favorite waters.

Where No Nonsense Guides Come From

No Nonsense guidebooks give you a quick, clear understanding of the essential information needed to learn a new fishing method or to fish a region's most outstanding waters. The authors are highly experienced in the techniques presented.

All who produce No Nonsense Guides believe in providing top quality products at a reasonable price. We also believe that all information should be verified. So we never hesitate to go out, rod in hand, to verify the facts and figures that appear in the pages of these guides. The staff is committed to this research.

It's hard work but we're glad to do it for you.

Jeff Suber, founder of The Forgotten Coast Kayak Anglers Club, chases birds against the Tampa skyline.

Even urban areas, such as Jamaica Bay in New York City, can be kayak fishing Meccas.

Table of Contents

Getting Started in Kayak Fishing

Let's Go Fishing

Photo by Connie Parrish.

Photo courtesy of Michael Maxwell.

Favorite Fishing Locations

Resources

Photo by Ryan Anderson.

About the Author

Cory Routh is an avid angler and environmentalist from Virginia Beach, Virginia, where he lives with his wife Cheryl, daughter Cara, and stepson Jeremy. He is a graduate of East Carolina University with a bachelor's degree in marine biology. After graduation he worked as a fisheries technician for the Virginia Department of Game and Inland Fisheries (VADGIF), maintaining and operating electrofishing gear on some of Virginia's warm water fisheries.

After a short stint with VADGIF, Cory accepted a permanent position in fisheries management with the Virginia Marine Resources Commission (VMRC). He was responsible for field collection of fisheries data used for resource management. His main responsibility was to remove the otoliths (ear bones) from several species of fish. These were used to calculate the age of the fish. After three years Cory was promoted to Senior Fisheries Management Specialist and charged with the administration of the Virginia Saltwater Recreational Fishing Development Fund program. This program funded several fishing projects such as public access, artificial reefs, fisheries research, and law enforcement. Because of his forward thinking and commitment to the program, he was awarded VMRC's Distinguished Service Award in 2003.

After seven years of service to VMRC, he accepted a position as Water Quality Specialist with the City of Virginia Beach. He remained with the city for three years monitoring the quality of its municipal water supply.

In 2007 Cory returned to state service with the Virginia Department of Environmental Quality (VADEQ). With DEQ, Cory is part of a team charged with monitoring environmental water quality. He runs various vessels, from 13 feet to 25 feet, and can be found on both fresh and saltwater water bodies throughout the Tidewater area of Virginia.

Nationally knows as "Ruthless," Cory has been a leader in the kayak fishing community. He was an original member of Wilderness Systems Kayak Fishing Team. Ruthless has competed in several tournaments from New York City to south Texas. With Team Wildy, he fished in the Extreme Edge Kayak Fishing Tournament series and in 2004 was named its Mid-Atlantic Kayak Angler of the Year. In 2005 Cory joined the Legacy Paddlesports team. He uses their brands, Heritage Kayaks and Native Watercraft, in all his adventures. He is also a pro-staffer for St. Croix Rods, Rip Tide Lures, Lateral Line, Northwest River Supply (NRS), and AT Paddles.

Photo by Francois Betoulaus.

Ruthless has fished waters from near his Virginia home to the East and Gulf Coasts to Hawaii. Cory has written several kayak fishing articles for *The Chesapeake Angler* and has given many presentations at national fishing shows and for angling clubs. He is the founder of the Tidewater Kayak Anglers Association (TKAA), one of the Mid-Atlantic's biggest kayak fishing communities. He also started their annual kayak fishing tournament, which is one of the biggest kayak fishing tournaments in the U.S. Their Web site is listed in the resources section.

Cory is owner-operator of Ruthless Fishing Inc., and guides kayak fishing adventures on his home waters in Virginia Beach. Ruthless is working on several kayak fishing projects and can be e-mailed at cory@ruthlessfishing.com. His Web site www.ruthlessfishing.com provides more information.

Cory, employed by the Virginia Department of Environmental Quality, conducts water quality sampling. Photo by Wick Harlan.

Cory gives many seminars throughout the year. At the Virginia Fly Fishing Festival, Cory's seminar was interpreted into sign language for the hearing impaired. Photo by Jim Shank.

The author with a Port St. Lucie sheepshead caught on a live shrimp. Photo by Francois Betoulaud.

Dedication

This book is dedicated to my wife Cheryl, my daughter Cara, my stepson Jeremy, and my parents. Thanks for putting up with my "Habitual Fishing Disorder" and having the patience to help me get through it.

The author and his daughter enjoy some quality time in the kayak. Photo by Sarah Jackson.

The author's tournament-ready kayak. He would rather have it and not need it, than need it and not have it.

Acknowledgments

I don't know where to start. So many folks have helped to make this happen. First and most important are my family—your support and patience are really what helped make this book happen. A special thank you to my father. I could not ask for a better business partner. I would like to thank Beau Beasley for pushing me to do this book. Beau has been an important friend and consultant on fishing, family, and life in general. You are like a brother to me. I would like to thank Wilderness Systems and specifically Harry Longerbeam. You had faith in me and were instrumental in getting me where I am today. To the original members of the Wildy Kayak Fishing Team, especially Dean Thomas, Scott Null, Ruben Garza, Phil Perry, and Joe Poole, you guys took in a fellow kayak angler and taught me the ropes. I learned a lot and got to fish some truly great locations and I can't thank you enough. I would like to thank Rick Roberts for organizing the Extreme Edge Kayak Fishing Tournaments. Even though these tournaments no longer exist, you started a network that continues to promote the sport.

I want to thank Andy Zimmerman, Mike Hooks, and Jimbo Meador of Legacy Paddlesports. You guys took me in and I have not regretted the move. You have done great things for the sport and I can't wait to see what the future holds. I am proud to be a part of the Legacy! I would also like to thank Chad Hoover. It has been an honor and a pleasure to travel and fish with you. I could not ask for a better fishing partner. I would like to thank the members of the Tidewater Kayak Anglers Association. The TKAA has been very instrumental in the promotion of the sport and taking it to the next level. Big props to "Kayak Kevin" Whitley and Ric Burnley for putting the sport on the map. I would also like to thank Mark Lozier for his help and input—you are a true friend and asset to Ruthless Fishing Inc.

A big thanks to Joe and Lillie Gilbert at Wild River Outfitters and to Tom Detrick and Vic Sorensen at Appomattox River Company. Both of these Virginia retailers have made great efforts to support kayak fishing, as well as my business. I would not be in this position had it not been for the support of both stores. If you are ever in Eastern Virginia, I highly suggest you check them out.

Thanks to Howard Fisher, Doug Goewey, Morenci Clark, and staff at No Nonsense Guides. Thanks for putting this project together. Last but not least, I would like to thank all those who helped out with pictures. May you be immortalized forever in this book! And to those who I forgot, please accept my apologies and I guess I'll owe you a drink when we next meet.

Tight Lines!
Cory "Ruthless" Routh

Author with a nice redfish from waters near Hickory Mound Unit, Big Bend WMA in Florida. Photo by Mark Lozier.

The author fighting a Lynnhaven Inlet redfish from his Ultimate 14.5 kayak. Photo by Wayne Bradby.

Foreword

by Beau Beasley

Coast to coast and everywhere in between, kayakers have taken the recreational world by storm. For some of these intrepid outdoors folk, the kayak is a means to an end, enabling them to put some distance between themselves and their cell phones. For others, kayaking is the end itself, and they live for the leisurely paddle, with or without companions.

The rest of us stand on the bank and watch the kayaker drift by and think, I sure would like to try that someday. And many of us do, marching into a local sporting goods store, plunking down (a lot of) hard-earned cash for a brand-new outfit, and driving home with a shiny new—and sometimes very large—toy. Each sunny day presents an opportunity—and yet, because we know nothing about kayaking, we don't know where to begin.

Cory Routh's *Kayak Fishing: The Complete Guide* is exactly where those new to kayaks should begin. From my first on-the-water experience with Cory—at Lynnhaven Inlet, Virginia—I recognized him as a man on a mission: Cory Routh seeks to demystify kayaks and kayak fishing and develop as many new devotees of the sport as possible. At the same time, he is committed to educating new anglers about their responsibility to protect the environment—particularly Virginia's fragile saltwater environs. He is a popular guide, a sought-after speaker, an acknowledged expert kayak fisherman, and a true friend to the novice kayaking angler.

Cory's unpretentious, step-by-step approach guides readers from selecting the right kayak, to loading and unloading their kayaks, to making the most of their time on the water regardless of their individual pursuits.

I think we can all agree that we need a little peace and quiet and a chance to reconnect with the outdoors. What better way to find that serenity than in a kayak on the water. Some kayak enthusiasts prefer to drown out rush hour by shooting the rapids or dodging rock gardens in whitewater. Others choose to meander down watery byways and camp out under the stars. Still others live to float a nearby river or shoreline, fishing rod in hand. For all of these kayakers, novice to advanced, *Kayak Fishing: The Complete Guide* is a great place to start.

Beau Beasley covering the 2006 TKAA kayak fishing tournament.

Beau Beasley
Author/Outdoor Photographer
Warrenton, Virginia

Kayak fishing is the fastest growing section of the paddlesports industry. Some even say it may have breathed new life into paddlesports.

Introduction

Francois Betoulaud with a nice skinny water snook.

This work is an accumulation of more than ten years of kayak fishing experience. In my travels I have had a wonderful opportunity to fish in some world-class kayak fishing locations, and with some of the best anglers in the sport. I have learned so much that I feel that if I don't write it down, I might forget. My goal is to make this one of the most complete kayak fishing guides available. The techniques in this book are proven, but are by no means the only way to do things. Feel free to modify anything to fit your personal preferences, just keep safety in mind. This book was written for both the beginner and seasoned kayak angler. It should be both educational and enjoyable.

I have kayak-fished the East and Gulf Coasts from New York City to Corpus Christi, Texas. My extensive research on kayak fishing has been hard work, and worth every last minute. I also give due credit to the individuals and resources who are listed in the back of this book. They have provided a myriad of information to supplement my personal experiences. I believe I have created a book

Chris Ellinson with a flounder from Lynnhaven Inlet.

worthy of its title, but I am an angler first, then a writer. We all make mistakes, and I alone accept all responsibility for any made in this book.

How To Use this Book

This book was written with all types and skill levels of anglers in mind. The information in these pages is valuable to all anglers whether they own a kayak or not. If you are a beginner it will put you on the right path—if you are seasoned it may teach you a new technique. I will walk you through the complete process of becoming a kayak angler. From choosing the right kayak—or two—to finding a knowledgable guide, it is all right here in these pages.

Rules and Regulations

At one time I had fishing licenses for nine different states, which meant that I had to be versed in nine different sets of regulations. Catch and release helps buffer the laws a little, but you should make an effort to know the rules that apply where you are fishing and whether a special permit or license is required. Most states have Web sites that sell licenses and offer up-to-date regulations. Nothing ruins a trip more than a "bad citation" from a warden. I remember hearing a saying that goes "ignorance of the law is no excuse," so be sure to study—there might be a test.

Conservation

I am a conservationist by nature and by education. As a ten-year employee of various conservation agencies, I am strongly committed to conserving natural resources. I believe that everyone must do his or her part to preserve natural resources, whether it is fish, submerged vegetation, or access areas. Everything helps, whether it is volunteering to plant sea grass or simply picking up a floating plastic bag. I believe that you should take conservation one step beyond what the law requires. I want my children and grandchildren to enjoy kayak fishing. As many know, I strongly advocate catch and release, but I have no problem whatsoever with reasonable catch and eat.

Safety

I am dedicated to safety as much as I am to conservation. Every concept in this book will consider safety first. As with any other sport, the first step is to know your personal limitations. The second is to not exceed them. Education is the best way to get ahead of the curve. There are many resources out there to help. Taking a basic paddling skills course with an ACA certified instructor is a great place

Ed Mears prepares to land a nice redfish.

to start. Having the right safety equipment is also important. I cannot stress enough how much of a difference it makes when you have the right gear.

Guides and Instructors

The absolute best place to learn the basics of kayak fishing is from licensed and insured guides and instructors. Most guides provide all the equipment, so you can actually "try it before you buy it," to make sure kayak fishing is for you. There is a an extensive listing in the guide resources section. These individuals have had training to ensure you have a safe and enjoyable trip. Yes it may cost more, but the knowledge you will gain from these professionals is invaluable. Being insured also protects you and the guide in the event of an accident.

Retailers

Another great place to get info on kayak fishing, kayaks, and equipment is your local retailer. Specialty stores are the best as they are geared specifically towards kayaking. Many shops even have kayak anglers on staff to point you in the right direction. Sometimes shops also have on-the-water demo days when you can talk to manufacturers' reps and try out their latest gear.

Clubs and Organizations

Even though the sport is relatively new, there are lots of kayak fishing organizations popping up around the nation. These clubs are a great place to learn specific kayak fishing techniques and even to meet a new fishing buddy or two. There is a complete listing of kayak fishing organizations in the resources section.

World Wide Web

If you run a search on "kayak fishing" on any Internet search engine you will get about a million results. This can be somewhat confusing. The best approach is to be very specific with the type of kayak fishing you want to do. That should narrow your search down to a more reasonable number of results. I have listed some of the most popular sites in the resources section.

Paddle sport retailers are the best places to start asking about kayak fishing.

Kayak angler Wayne Bradby "eeling" for trophy striped bass off of the Eastern shore of Virginia.

Mark Lozier getting the upper hand on a Florida redfish.

Cody Hinkle of Virginia Beach with his first catch from a kayak.

The author's Magic 14.5 rigged for solo fishing. The Magic can be paddled solo or tandem.

Getting Started in Kayak Fishing

Photo by Ryan Anderson.

Why Kayak Fishing?

Probably one of the most avid young anglers I know, Drew Letourneau holds up two nice Atlantic Croakers.

The answer to this question can span more pages than I plan on writing. I personally find kayak fishing more than appealing for many reasons. From conservation, to affordability, to portability, kayak fishing has many advantages that far outweigh any disadvantages.

Conservation

With the exception of making you a more effective angler, kayaking has almost no impact on the environment. You are not burning gas, so there are no emissions. There is very little impact on sensitive habitats such as sea grass and oyster bars. Kayaks can operate in mere inches of water and still not impact the bottom. Kayaks are quiet with the exception of the occasional "woo hoo" from an angler being pulled around by a big fish.

Affordability

If you are a boat owner you can relate to the "hole in the water to put money in" concept. If you took the taxes that you pay for just putting fuel in your motor boat, you can probably take that money and buy a fully rigged kayak. With a kayak, all the fuel you need is a RC Cola and a moon pie. Kayaks are the perfect way for folks who cannot afford boats to get onto the water. With kayaks there are no hidden costs. Your initial investment (unless you are a gadget junkie) is all the money you will have to put into your equipment. On average you can get kayak, paddle, and PFD for about $1,000.

Portability

Kayaks obviously take up less space than conventional boats and they also weigh a lot less. If you can walk down to the water, you can launch a kayak there. Kayaks can be carried on car tops, in truck beds, on trailers, or even behind bicycles. A lot of the headaches you have with a motorboat are not there with kayaks. Many times I launch at crowded boat ramps by walking my kayak to areas where the boat trailers cannot go. A set of kayak wheels is a good investment, and make getting your kayak from your vehicle to the water much easier.

Accessibility

Kayaks are often referred to as "the best waders you will ever own." Even hard-core wade fishermen are using kayaks to access shallow areas that they cannot reach by walking. Deep water and boot sucking muddy bottoms are not issues to wade anglers who use kayaks. Surf fishermen are also reaping the benefits of kayaking by paddling out baits farther than they can cast. You can launch a kayak anywhere you can access the water. Ideally, all you need is a sandy beach. There are many public access areas that do not have formal boat launches and these are the areas where kayaks rule.

Maintenance

Basically all you need to fix a plastic kayak is a roll of good duct tape. Rotomolded polyethylene kayaks are practically indestructible. And, if you do get a hole, it may be repairable by your local retailer. If you take care of your kayak, it will last several years, or at least until something new comes along, and you get an upgrade. Everyday scratches from boat ramps, shells, etc., are nothing more than aesthetic and typically will not affect hull integrity. Just a simple clean, fresh water rinse is all you need to do, while a little detergent may be used to remove any "fishy" odors and stains. Opening up your hatches while in storage and airing them out will also help keep your kayak from getting a skunky smell.
To protect your kayak from UV rays and keep it looking new, spray it with 303 Protectant. You can pick some up at most kayak retailers.

One big advantage of kayaking is the access to tight fishing spots, like shopping mall goldfish ponds. Photo by Beau Beasley.

Before You Start

Ruthless trying out his Redfish 12 in Lynnhaven inlet. This is his preferred kayak for clients of his business. Photo by Matt Routh.

Before we look at kayaks, I recommend you take the following steps to make sure that you are thoroughly ready for kayak fishing.

What's up Doc?

Just like any exercise program, you should get a checkup from your doctor prior to starting, to tell if kayaking is for you and whether you should go in full steam, or take it slowly. Either way, do what the doctor tells you. Then return after six months and see what a difference a kayak fishing workout makes.

Back to School

There are instructors out there who can teach you proper paddle and rescue techniques. The best instructors are certified by the American Canoe Association (ACA). Their instructors go through a rigorous training regimen to ensure you are taught the latest and most effective paddling techniques. Most paddle shops and outfitters have an ACA-certified instructor on staff and offer several basic paddling technique classes throughout the year.

These same instructors can also instruct you in what to do if things go wrong and you capsize. It is a good idea to practice capsizing and recoveries with an instructor at first, then continue to practice in controlled environments. See your local outfitters for more info. The ACA Web site is www.americancanoe.org.

Outfitters

Visit your local outfitter and talk with their paddling experts. They should be able to point you in the right direction. Some outfitters even have an angler available on staff.

The Club Scene

There is not a better place to learn the basics of kayak fishing than a local kayak fishing club. There are several clubs located around the country and the world. See the Resources section for a listing of kayak fishing clubs. Attend a monthly meeting, a seminar, or check out their Web sites. There is a wealth of information out there, and who better to learn from than your fellow kayak anglers.

Kayak fishing seminars are a great place to learn about the sport.

Larry Routh on the hunt for big fish in Deep River, located in Worthville, North Carolina. Photo by Connie Parrish.

Safety and Self-rescues

Intentionally capsizing your kayak in a controlled environment is great practice for the inevitable "turtle." The author takes his Manta Ray 14 to the point of no return. Photo by Vic Sorensen.

The key to a safe kayak fishing trip is having the confidence in your equipment and skills. The more you learn the better kayak angler you will become. Knowing how to handle an incident, whether it be a "turtle" or an imbedded fishing hook, can make a difference. In this section I will go over the equipment you should have and skills you should know to be prepared for whatever kayak fishing can dish out.

Kayak Modifications for Safety

There are a few things you can do to make your kayak safer.

1. Add extra floatation, such as pool noodles, to your interior storage if you are going to be fishing in open water. This can make all the difference if you get into trouble.
2. Stick reflective tape on the hull and on your paddle blades. This will make you more visible to rescuers with search lights.

3. In permanent ink or with an engraver, write your name, phone number, and address on the inside of your kayak. If you are separated from your kayak, rescuers will be able to ID the kayak and know where and if they need to search for you. It also helps with recovery if your kayak is stolen. Write down the hull ID number and store it in a safe place.

Mandatory Safety Equipment

PFD

There are a few things that, according to the USCG, must be on a kayak. First, you must have a Personal Flotation Device (PFD). Most kayakers use a Type III PFD. I suggest you get a paddle-specific vest from one of the many manufacturers out there. These PFDs are cut for comfort and designed with the paddler in mind. The key is to buy a PFD that you will actually wear. We have a rule in the TKAA, and that is "if you are paddling, you should wear your PFD." There are models with various pockets and accessory loops that are designed for anglers. A good example is the Chinook by NRS. It has lots of storage and is ventilated. It also has a high back to accommodate the seating found on most Sit On Top (SOT) kayaks.

A Type III PFD that is paddle specific is your best bet. The Chinook by NRS is a great choice.

All PFDs must be approved by the USCG or other entity. Most PFDs should have a similar label in the back.

Lights

The coast guard has a minimum requirement here. They specify all you need is a simple white light, such as a flashlight, or head lamp. This light must be readily accessible to warn other boaters of your position. I suggest you go further and, in addition to the flashlight, purchase or make a 360-degree light. The 360 light is a simple white light that can be seen 360 degrees around the vessel. On a kayak it must be at the highest point and not obscured by anything, including the paddler's head. Avoid use of the red/green navigation light on a kayak, this indicates a motorized vessel. With the advent of LED lights you

There are many 360-degree lights available. These LED 360 lights, to be used with Scotty rod holder brackets, were designed by the author.

If you plan on fishing at night you should have a good 360-degree light. This is an ideal set up. Notice the light is unobstructed and above the angler's head.

can get hundreds of hours out of one set of batteries. I also suggest you purchase a LED headlamp. It can serve as a back up if your 360 light goes out. Carry an extra set of batteries, just in case.

Noise Making Device

This category includes whistles, horns, and bells. The most simple and portable is the whistle. There are several models out there. Look for whistles that are labeled SOLAS and are "pealess." The whistles with peas tend to fail more than the pealess ones. Another option is an air horn. There are several types out there from breath powered, to aerosol, to compressed air. These are good and take up less space but have limited shelf life on a kayak.

All three items can be combined to make a system that will pass most marine safety inspections for a kayak. I fasten my whistle and flashlight to my PFD with a short piece of Niteline (reflective rope). This way everything that is required stays with me, as long as I am wearing my PFD.

Float Plan

Someone should know where you are going and how long you will be gone. I consider this very important. Whether you simply tell someone or fill out a complete float plan, this simple step can make the difference in how long it takes rescuers to find you. I always fill out a simple form just in case the person I tell doesn't remember the details. Every time you go kayak fishing, file a float plan with a family member and keep another copy on the dash of your vehicle. The float plan should include the following information for every member of the group:

- Name, age, and experience level
- Kayak color and type
- Clothing and vital medical information
- Emergency contact information
- Launch time and location
- Take out time, location, and date of return
- Route planned and camping spots
- Safety equipment onboard
- Vehicle type(s), license plate number(s), and parking location

Recommended Safety Equipment

When it comes to safety equipment, I like the saying "I would rather have it and not need it, than need it and not have it." Even though the following items are optional, I highly recommend you consider them for all your kayak adventures.

First Aid Kit

Whether it is simple or well stocked, a first aid kit should be included in your gear. There are several prepackaged kits from $10 and up or you can build your own. Just make sure to have the basics. I prefer to buy these since most are sealed and contain everything I need. These are easy to store in a dry box. Once opened, I resupply as needed and make sure to check expiration dates, especially on medications. Here are some basic items to include in your kit:

- Waterproof Band-Aids® in assorted sizes
- Triple antibiotic ointment
- Gauze pads (4 inch square)
- Gauze roll (3 inches wide)
- Medical tape (1 inch wide)
- Needle for removing splinters or opening blisters
- Moleskin for treating blisters
- Small bottle of disinfectant soap or cleansing towelettes
- Tweezers
- Razor blade or small folding scissors
- Dental floss
- Large bandana to use as sling
- Loop of 50-lb mono for hook removal
- 6-inch wire cutters for cutting hooks

Additionally, you can add the following items and over-the-counter medications:

- Space blanket
- Waterproof matches in waterproof container or a lighter
- Chapstick and sunscreen
- Bug repellant
- Super glue
- Analgesic pain killer (ibuprofen or acetaminophen)
- Antihistamine (Benadryl for bites, poison ivy, etc.)
- Antacid

Rescue Knife

There are many types of rescue knives available. I use the rescue hook by Benchmade. This knife consists of a ring that your finger goes through that is attached to a very sharp hook shaped blade. It is designed specifically for cutting rope or cord. It is not as dangerous as a fixed blade knife, and will not cause accidental damage to you or your kayak. Blunt-tip dive knives are handy and less likely to cause injury or damage. Keep your rescue knife accessible.

The Benchmade rescue hook is perfect for cutting lines in an emergency. Its design is compact and easy to use.

One of the main disadvantages of a Sit In Kayak (SINK) is that you will have to get the water out of the cockpit. This can be accomplished on the water with a hand pump and a sponge.

Paddle Float/ Rescue Sling

If you anticipate difficulty in getting back in your kayak, you should purchase a paddle float and a sling. The sling consists of a simple nylon loop that is used to assist in reentering your kayak. The paddle float is a device that turns your paddle into an outrigger to help stabilize your kayak. It also makes a great secondary floatation if needed. There is a description on how to use these later in this section.

Bilge Pump and Sponge

Even the SOT kayaks take on a little water and you will need an effective way to remove it. A sponge is an excellent dewatering tool if space is limited. I also carry a hand bilge pump which is better for removing larger volumes of water.

Visual Distress Markers

These include flares, dye markers, smoke, and flags. Let's face it—kayaks are hard to see. So if you are trying to signal for aid, you need every advantage possible. These items increase visibility and get you rescued quicker.

A good deck bag is great for carrying items you need to grab quickly. This kit by NRS contains a hand pump, sponge, paddle float, signal mirror, and a whistle.

Tow Rig

A tow rig is designed to allow one paddler to tow another. It usually consists of a belt attached to a bag that contains a length of floating rope and a hook. There are many other uses for this piece of gear and it is very handy to have.

Survival/Ditch Kit

This is a dry bag that contains everything I think I would need in a survival situation. The items vary according to the trip. It contains my first-aid kit, various survival items, and a change of dry clothes. In an emergency situation this is the first thing I will grab, and I keep it in a handy place.

Extra Paddle

This is self explanatory. I keep an extra two-piece paddle in my kayak. You wouldn't want to be up the creek...well, you know the rest.

Communications (Marine VHF, Cell Phone)

I consider my handheld marine VHF radio one of my most valuable pieces of equipment. I use the Uniden Voyager, which is waterproof, and small enough to fit in the pockets of my PFD. In an emergency it is the best way to call for help. (The USCG always monitors channel 16.) It is also a valuable tool to communicate with other anglers, as well as listen in on "where the bite is happening." Most kayak anglers have adopted VHF channel 72 as their main channel of communication. Cell phones are life savers. Preprogram the phone numbers of your local rescue agencies ahead of time. Keep your cell phone in a waterproof container such as a dry bag. There are dry bags available that allow you to operate the phone without removing it from the container. Some cellular phone companies are making waterproof phones.

Compass

Whether you use a handheld or deck-mounted compass, knowing your bearings can keep you from paddling around in circles. I keep my compass in a waterproof map bag along with charts of the area where I am going to fish. Having a deck-mounted compass allows you to paddle without having to hold onto it. Always trust your compass.

Rescues

This section is not a replacement to taking a lesson with a certified ACA instructor. It is simply for reference. I highly recommend you practice with an experienced instructor and in a controlled environment. Check out the ACA Web site for an instructor in your area. Due to the popularity of SOT kayaks, I choose to show rescues using these kayaks. However, the techniques are similar for both types of kayaks.

Kayak anglers never think that they will ever "turtle" or capsize their kayak. They learn early on that even with the most stable kayak they are still prone to turtle. It is important to know how to rig your kayak to prevent loss of equipment, but it is even more important to know how to protect your most important asset, your life. Whether you paddle SOT or SINK kayaks, learning rescues is the most important skill you can know.

Taking a class with an instructor is the best way to learn rescue techniques.

Belly, Butt, and Feet Technique

This is the most common way to recover from a capsized SOT kayak. The design of the SOT allows it to be relatively waterproof and self-bailing. All you need to do is to right the kayak, secure any displaced gear, and get back on the kayak. In the following demonstration below, ACA instructor Vic Sorensen, of www.kayakinstruction.us, shows us how.

The first step is to capsize. Try to get a feel for your kayak's initial and secondary stability and to find its "point of no return." Think about how you are going to enter the water. Always try to keep a hand on your kayak and your paddle.

Once you pass the point of no return, you have a successful "turtle." Not all incidents overturn the kayak, but if it capsizes you have to get it righted.

Right your kayak by getting your shoulder under the gunwales and pushing it up and over. In some cases, you may need to reach under to the other side and pull it towards you as you lift the side closest to you.

Always keep a hand on your kayak so it does not get away from you.

Stabilize your kayak and make sure to clear the deck of any objects that may get in the way. Retrieve your paddle and prepare to pull yourself onto the kayak.

Unless you have a paddle leash, keep one hand on the paddle so it does not get away from you.

With the hand that is closest to the seat, grab the far side grab handle and pull yourself onto the kayak. Kick your legs so they come to the surface. The idea is to achieve an angle that assists in pulling your belly across the kayak.

The key is to center your belly button over the seat. Be sure to keep low to the kayak. The higher your center of gravity, the more likely you will capsize again.

Keep one hand on each side of the seat and rotate your butt into the seat. With your feet still in the water, stabilize the kayak.

Swing your legs into the kayak and put them in the foot wells. Stabilize the kayak and organize your gear.

Paddle Float and Sling

If you have difficulty getting back into your kayak, consider using a paddle float and a sling. A paddle float is an inflatable pocket that fastens over your paddle and is used as an outrigger to help stabilize the kayak. Used in conjunction with a sling, it becomes a tool that greatly assists in getting you back in your kayak. Again I have Vic show us how to use the paddle float and sling.

I cannot stress enough how important learning these rescue techniques can be. Not two weeks after taking a rescue class, I was caught in 70-mph winds and literally blown off of my kayak. I was amazed how quickly I recovered. I also realized that I was not wearing my PFD. Now I always practice rescues and ALWAYS wear my PFD.

Retrieve your paddle float and slide it over the blade of your paddle. Secure it with the attached hardware.

Inflate the paddle float and check to make sure it stays on your paddle.

Slip the rescue sling over the opposite blade and reach it across the deck of the kayak.

Reach under the kayak and pull the opposite end of the sling to your side of the kayak.

Wrap the loose end of the sling around the paddle shaft until you have enough length to get your foot in.

Insert your foot into the loop you created and step up onto the kayak.

Get your belly button over the seat and be sure to keep your center of gravity low.

Rotate around and sit in the seat.

Swing your legs into the kayak.

Retrieve your float and sling. Keep the float inflated and at the ready until you are in safer waters.

Choosing a Kayak

Choosing the right kayak can be very confusing. Talking to your local outfitter can get you into the fishing kayak that best suits you.

Choosing the Right Kayak

Every year more and more kayak manufacturers are catering to anglers. This has made choosing a fishing kayak very difficult for the beginner. When I started there were no kayaks specifically for anglers and now there are several to choose from. Where do you start? Well, that will depend on a few things. First, how much are you planning to spend? Second, what kinds of fishing are you planning to do and where? And third, how do you plan to transport and store the kayak? By considering these factors you can make an educated decision and find your perfect angling kayak.

How Much Is That Kayak?

Your budget will determine which kayak you will buy. Used kayaks may be cheaper and may already be rigged out, but you may buy a lemon, or in nautical terms, a banana. If you find a used kayak, always water test it first, and even have an experienced paddler check it out. Newer boats will be shiny and the color will be vivid. Watch out for dents, cracks, and faded areas. The faded areas are where the boat was exposed to UV and if put under pressure, may crack and leak. Good places for used kayaks are outfitters, most rotate their demo and rental kayaks every year. Your best bet is to buy a new kayak. It may cost more, but most new kayaks include customer service and warranties against defects. With kayaks, you definitely get what you pay for. Quality plastics, resins, and stainless hardware cost more, therefore increasing production cost. That being said, there are several quality kayaks out there that retail for less than $500. These are great kayaks for beginners. Also think about accessories, a quality paddle-specific PFD and paddle can cost almost as much as a kayak, but remember that these can be used with your next kayak if you decide to upgrade.

How and Where Am I Going to Fish?

Not all kayaks are created equal. They come in about every shape and size, just like people. Not all kayaks are suited to all types of fishing. Short wide boats are more maneuverable and stable, but tend not to track well. Longer narrow boats are faster and track well, but are less stable. If you are an angler who wants to fish small protected areas, a shorter boat will work. Shorter boats also work well in flowing rivers, where maneuverability is preferred to speed. But if you plan to cover lots of open water, longer faster kayaks are preferable.

Who best to match a specific type of kayak to fishing than professional guides? One example is Jeff Little of Blue Ridge Kayak Fishing. He mostly fishes flowing fresh water rivers with some white water, and he prefers the Tarpon 100 for his type of fishing. Its shorter length and maneuverability makes it the perfect SOT for chasing smallmouth and other river species.

Another example is Dean "Slowride" Thomas of Slowride Charters. Slowride fishes tidal flats and marshes around Aransas Pass, Texas. Dean covers lots of shallow, open water while chasing tailing redfish. He prefers the speedy and straight tracking Tarpon 140 and 160i kayaks.

In my business, Ruthless Fishing, I fish a combination of waters from the open water of the Atlantic Ocean to the shallow tributaries of the Chesapeake Bay. Not all kayaks will work for everyone, and there are some limitations that every potential kayak angler must be aware of, such as weight. Bigger anglers must be aware of the kayak's weight capacity. Consider your weight plus at least 10-20 pounds of fishing gear when looking at kayaks. Another limitation is your paddling ability. I suggest a beginner go for the slow and stable kayaks. Eventually, as you progress, you can move on to faster, sleeker kayaks.

How Do I Get It Home and Where Am I Gonna Put It?

Another deciding factor in choosing a kayak is how you plan to transport it, and when you get it home, where to put it. If you have a big SUV with roof racks, you can carry any kayak. However, if you drive a sub-compact car or a short bed truck, you may be better off with a smaller kayak. I find that most beginners with storage and transportation limitations are better off with 12-foot kayaks. These will fit in most apartments and garages, and can fit into the bed of smaller trucks. Also the 12-footers are still long enough to give ideal paddling characteristics for angling. The 12-footers are definitely the best size when you consider transportation, storage, and performance. I discuss the finer points of kayak transportation and storage later in the book.

I hope this helps you find that perfect kayak. If you are still confused, the best place to go is to your local outfitter or guide service. Most outfitters have demo days that allow potential paddlers to try as may different kayaks as they can. Go to one of these demos, ask a lot of questions, and try out the kayaks. There are always experts on hand who can help you pick the right one. Some demos invite kayak anglers to bring their rigged kayaks, so always be on the lookout for them.

SOT vs. SINK

For kayak fishing there are two basic hull designs available.

The first is the Sit In Kayak or SINK. This is the style most people associate with kayaking and stems from the traditional style used by the Eskimos. By design, the paddler sits inside the kayak and the center of gravity is lower. This allows the kayak to be narrow, yet maintain stability. SINK hull designs range from sleek touring styles to wider recreational kayaks such as Native Watercraft's

Even Sit In Kayaks can be rigged for successful fishing.

Marvel. These recreational kayaks have larger non-restricting cockpits and are more forgiving than touring kayaks. They are not suited for anglers who like to wade. The main disadvantage of a SINK is that if you do capsize the kayak will take on water, and it is more difficult to get back into. Only with proper training and practice can anglers master the recovery technique. This is the main reason self-bailing Sit On Top kayaks are preferred by anglers.

This brings me to the next type of kayak, the Sit On Top or SOT. This design has its roots in the need for a surf-worthy kayak that can take being swamped by waves yet still float. This self-bailing design also gained notoriety in the recreational paddling area because there was no need to learn the "Eskimo roll" rescue technique. Ocean Kayak is noted for designing one of the first fishing friendly kayaks in the Scupper Pro TW. The TW stands for tank well, which Ocean Kayak made bigger to accommodate larger cargos. This kayak became popular with the angling community and soon other companies, like Wilderness Systems, followed suit and developed fishing-specific kayaks. Wilderness Systems Tarpon kayak line started a design trend that is still followed by many other manufacturers. SOTs have many advantages and almost no disadvantages. The main disadvantage of a SOT is that you and your gear are more exposed to the elements. Modern SOTs continue to grow in popularity. As designs evolve and improve, so do the materials manufacturers are using.

Paddle or Pedal

Not all kayaks require you to paddle. Hobie has led the way by developing an efficient and powerful means to propel kayaks using foot power. This option has many advantages and has helped revolutionize the sport. The Hobie system is called MirageDrive. It uses a back-and-forth pedal motion to propel two wing-like fins. These fins look like the wings of penguins as they swim through the water. Each wing sweeps along the width of the kayak to produce a great amount of thrust. Native Watercraft is also producing a new pedal kayak. Their approach uses a more traditional rotational motion and shaft-driven propeller. This system is currently available on the Ultimate series of kayaks. Having hands-free ability with pedal-driven kayaks is a huge advantage for kayak fishing. Spend more time fishing and less time paddling. They are also a great choice for folks with limited upper body strength and mobility. The drawback is that the pedal drives extend well below the kayak and limit your draft. They are not as efficient in areas where the water is too shallow to fully extend them. However, you can always grab a paddle for traversing these areas.

Construction

Kayaks have come a long way from the skin on wood designs of long ago. Now most fishing kayaks are made of rotomolded polyethylene plastic. This material starts off as a grainy colored powder that is poured into a mold of a specific design. Decals are placed inside the mold and will adhere to the plastic as it adheres to the mold. The aluminum mold is then rotated and heated in a huge clam shell oven. The temperature and time vary for each mold and plastic. After the allotted time, the mold is removed from the oven and rotated over cooling fans. After cooling, the mold is opened to reveal a shiny virgin kayak. When the kayak cools to room temperature it is inspected and then outfitted with hatches and hardware. After a final inspection the kayak is stored upright until it is shipped to your local outfitter.

Plastic kayaks are very durable, but tend to be heavier than fiberglass and Kevlar kayaks. Some manufacturers are making composite fishing kayaks, however, their cost is substantially higher. Companies such as Hurricane Aquasports use a different molding process to make lighter, more rigid kayaks. They use the thermo molding method to create their kayaks. Legacy Paddlesports has taken an even higher tech approach to making lighter kayaks. They have partnered with Milliken to

Al Stillman, of East Coast Kayak Fishing, fights a Florida redfish from a Hobie Revolution kayak.

PFDs and Paddles

My NRS Chinook is the most important piece of safety equipment, so I always wear it. Because it has lots of storage, it also carries all my mandatory and optional safety equipment. In the larger pockets I carry a whistle, waterproof LED light, and a signal mirror. These items are attached to a lanyard that is then attached to the vest. In the big pocket I carry my waterproof VHF radio. In the smaller top pockets I carry my waterproof cell phone and waterproof digital camera. The rescue hook is attached to the left shoulder strap and a blunt dive knife to the straps under my arm. Add a good pair of floating pliers like the XTOOLS® Hybrid and you are set. The nice thing about this setup is that no matter what kayak I paddle that day, I will pass any safety checks.

PFDs

Your personal floatation device, or PFD, is your most important piece of safety equipment. Wearing a properly fitted PFD can make the difference between life and death. The U.S. Coast Guard does not require you to wear a PFD. However, you should wear it whenever you're paddling. I wear my PFD at all times while in my kayak and remove it only if I can put my feet on the bottom when sitting in my kayak. Most kayakers like to simply put their PFDs under a bungee or keep them within reach. I challenge you to try and don a PFD when swimming in water too deep to wade. Here are a few steps to ensure you select the right PFD for your brand of kayak.

1. Try on the PFD in the store. Cinch up all the straps so the fit is snug but comfortable. Have another person pull up on the PFD. If it comes loose, readjust it, try another size, or select another model.
2. Sit in a kayak that is closest to the model you own. Most new kayakers buy a PFD at the same time as their kayak. This is a great opportunity to get a PFD that fits you and your kayak. If the PFD is uncomfortable or it rides up while sitting in the kayak, try readjusting the straps or try another model.
3. Buy a PFD that you truly like. If you own an ugly or ill-fitting PFD you probably won't wear it.

There are plenty of sharp looking kayak fishing-specific PFDs. Shop around to find the right one for you. Keep in mind that if you are going to kayak fish year-round, the PFD needs to be multi-seasonal. Choose a PFD that can be let out to accommodate the bulk of paddling wear.

Paddles

Other than your kayak and PFD, your paddle is one of the most important purchases you will make. There are several types of paddles out there, from wood to high-tech composites. The key is to go with the best paddle you can afford. The lighter the paddle the easier it is going to be on you after a long day. I suggest you look for paddles with composite or fiberglass shafts. Then, depending on your budget, choose plastic or composite blades. Paddle lengths for SOT kayaks vary from 210 to 245 cm. Getting the length just right is very important. As a rule of thumb, your height, weight, strength, and the width of your kayak should determine paddle length. If you are short, try a smaller paddle. If you are tall try longer paddles. Longer paddles tend to require more power and are less efficient than shorter paddles, which do not provide as much power. See the table for a range of paddle sizes.

A paddle with adjustable ferrules allows for length adjustment and blade angle, called feather. Blade size and shape also vary. I prefer oversized asymmetrical blades. These are commonly found on recreational paddles. I use the Fishstix paddle by Adventure Technology. It is a composite paddle with an ergonomic bent shaft and is absolutely the best paddle for kayak fishing. Adventure Technology also has a straight shaft paddle with polypropylene blades and fully adjustable ferrules. It is a great value for around $100. I treat paddles like my fishing equipment. Just like a strong fishing rod, a light strong paddle can be just as important. Bottom line, get a paddle that you can use comfortably, effectively, and most of all, the best one you can afford.

The author with an early version of the AT Fishstix paddle, and dinner. Photo by Robert Lienmann.

Choosing the right paddle to fit you is as important as picking the right kayak.

Paddler Height	Paddle Length (cm)
5'0"	215
5'3"	215
5'6"	220
5'9"	225
6'0"	230
6'3"	235

Adventure Technology suggests these guidelines when choosing a paddle for kayak fishing.

Kayak Rigging

Two fully rigged kayaks ready for a day on the water. Stickers are optional.

Now that you have picked out a kayak, what are your options as far as making it your dream fishing machine? Keep in mind that the following accessories can be used on both types of kayaks, Sit On Top (SOT) and Sit In Kayaks (SINK) and it is up to you to decide on which items work best for your kayak. Before cutting and drilling your kayak, I suggest that you measure and re-measure to make sure everything will work out just right. Check all your clearances before making anything permanent. Always use stainless steel machine screws, washers, and nylon lock (nyloc) nuts. On my boats, I lay everything out before permanently attaching anything to the kayak. This mock-up helps ensure that everything fits correctly and does not interfere with the operation (mainly the paddling) of the kayak.

Paddle Leashes and Holders

Paddle clips or holders are nice, especially if you plan to anchor when you fish. They allow you to stow your paddle in an easily accessible place (usually the side opposite from your casting side) while you fish. A paddle leash is also a nice accessory and will usually eliminate the need for a spare paddle. Paddle leashes should be removed for surf launches because you may become tangled in them if you capsize in the wash.

Backrests

Nearly all major manufacturers have comfortable seating as standard equipment. Legacy Paddlesports has set the bar with their First Class Seating™. Not every SOT comes with such comfortable seating. There are several companies who make aftermarket seating. Surf to Summit has an angler seat that includes a tackle pocket and rod holders. Keep in mind that adding a seat may change your center of gravity and affect the stability of your kayak.

Rod Holders

It is obvious that you cannot paddle your kayak and hold a fishing rod at the same time, so rod holders are one of the most important accessories that you add to your kayak. There are about as many types of rod holders as there are fishing rods. The two main types of holders are recessed (like on the gunnels of most boats) and trolling rod holders. Recessed holders are nice because they are flush and do

Paddle holders are handy when you need to store the paddle out of the way. Here they are still readily accessible.

Paddle leashes are a good form of insurance, especially if you have a high-end paddle.

A nice seat can make spending all day in a kayak more comfortable. Many manufacturers are integrating more comfortable seats into their kayaks.

Scotty makes a rod holder that will accommodate and secure every type of fishing rod.

Scotty also makes a fly rod holder, shown here.

Some kayaks may require extensions to make the rods more accessible.

Precision Pak® makes a great tackle storage system with integrated rod holders and lots of storage.

The Scotty Baitcast/Spincast rod holder model will accommodate both spinning and casting rods securely. It will hold fly rods but not as securely.

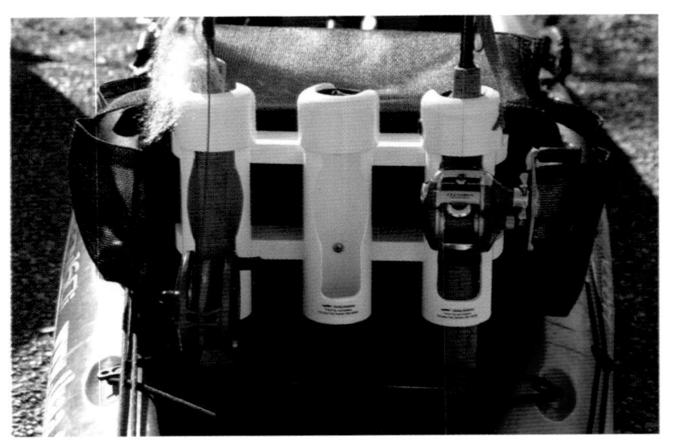

Here the author uses a crate system he helped design. He uses the rod holder by I Fly, which works with more than just fly rods.

not interfere with paddling, however, you cannot adjust the rod angle. When installed on a SOT, recessed holders must be capped to prevent water from entering dry storage inside the kayak. Trolling holders are usually adjustable and can be removed if they get in the way. Both types will require drilling for installation, however, recessed rod holders will require that a 2-inch hole be cut for installation. If you can get to the backside, use screws, washers, and nyloc nuts. If you cannot get inside, use stainless or aluminum blind rivets. Don't worry, drilling the first hole is always the hardest.

Anchors and Anchor Shuttles

There are several types of anchors. The most common anchors used for kayaking are the folding claw or grapple, Bruce, and stake out poles.

The claw anchor is a good all-around anchor that can be folded up for storage. It will work in nearly any condition with moderate to slow current. It is especially good in fresh water.

The Bruce or manta anchor is designed for muddy and sandy bottoms. This is my personal favorite and works well in saltwater.

The stake out pole is used in shallow water (up to 2 feet). It consists of a pole that is pushed into the bottom and attached to the anchor shuttle system. This is the quickest anchor to use and good for staking out the kayak when you decide to wade. About 50 to 100 feet of line should suffice for most kayak fishing applications. Keep in mind that because kayaks have little drag, they can be set with smaller anchors and less line scope. A good rule is that you should have three times as much rope as the water is deep. For example, you will need 30 feet of rope to hold in 10 feet of water.

The anchor shuttle is another handy accessory. It can be as complicated or as simple as you want it to be. Basically, it allows you to move your anchor connection to the front or the back of the kayak. By doing this you can maneuver your kayak into the optimum position for the type of fishing you are doing. My anchor shuttle consists of two pulleys, one at each end of the kayak. A line runs through both pulleys and forms a loop (like an old-time clothesline). I connect a clip to the line, and when I need to position my anchor line, I simply attach it to the clip and shuttle it where it needs go.

Anchor Rigging

All your anchors should be rigged so they can reverse if they get stuck. The claw and Bruce anchors have holes at the bottom that allow you to rig them this way. Use a small shackle to attach the rope to the bottom of the anchor, and then use a small cable tie to attach the rope to the end of the shaft of the anchor. Regular use will not break the tie. If the anchor is snagged, give a good yank, the tie will break and reverse the direction of the anchor. You should also install a float at the other end of the anchor line. This allows you to dump the anchor if necessary. You can always go back and get it later. If conditions get bad (currents, waves, etc.) dump the anchor and return when it is safe. You should never anchor in very fast current or in big swells.

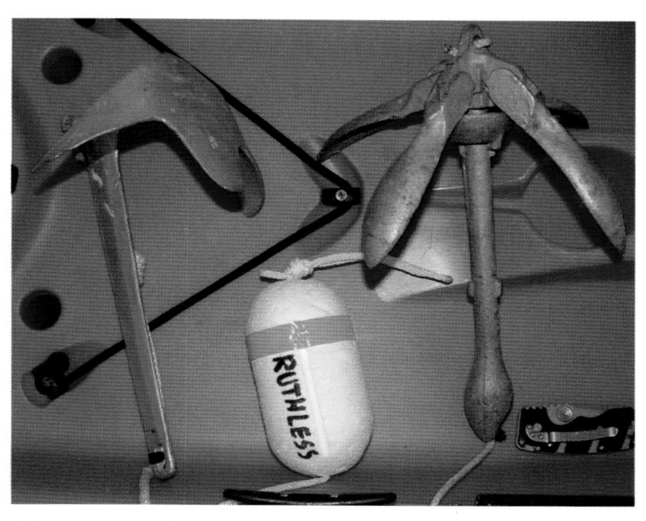

The most popular anchors are the Bruce or manta anchor, and the folding grapple anchor. Adding a float will make retrieval easier if you have to ditch the anchor in a pinch.

It is important to add a breakaway system to your kayak anchor, just in case it hangs up. Trying to retrieve a stuck anchor can lead to a turtle.

Watertrail Accessories has a prepackaged shuttle that comes with everything you need for installation.

Installing the Shuttle System

Step 1. Decide on which side to mount the shuttle. I prefer the side opposite of my casting hand. Attach the pulleys to the bow and stern of the kayak. Get them as close to the end as you can without interfering with other systems such as the rudder. You may have to use pad eyes and rivet them to the kayak. On most SOTs, you can attach the pulleys to the carrying handles at both ends of the kayak. Use bungee cord to attach the pulleys to the pad eyes or to the handles. I use hog rings to make a loop of bungee. This will keep the shuttle tight to the hull and absorb any shock associated with anchoring. (Figure 1)

Step 2. Run Niteline or 550 cord through the pulleys and make a loop in both ends of the line. Make sure the line is tight enough so that the bungee stretches and keeps the line taut. Connect these two loops using a stainless carabiner and a 2-inch stainless welded ring. I use hog rings and marine heat shrink to attach the ropes to the hardware. This makes a clean connection and allows the hardware to get closer to the pulleys. (Figure 2)

Step 3. Use heat or shrink tubing to clean up any tattered ends. (Figure 3)

Step 4. Install a small boat cleat at the midpoint of your kayak on the same side as the shuttle system. Using the ladder or zigzag cleat allows you to attach the anchor line from either direction, and allows for a quick release if you get into trouble. (Figure 4)

I will describe using anchors and shuttle systems in the Kayak Positioning and Maneuvering section.

Live Wells and Bait Buckets

For bait fishermen there needs to be a place to keep bait fresh or frisky. I have seen kayaks with live wells but I think this is a bit extravagant, yet there are ways to convert 5-gallon buckets into very effective aerated live wells. The problem is they need power and live well pumps can rapidly suck the life out of any battery small enough to carry on the kayak. My favorite way to keep bait alive is a simple trolling type bait bucket. There are several types that will fit most kayaks. To keep my bait alive I simply put it overboard. When I need to move it goes back in my tank well and I move on to the next fishing spot.

Installing a Shuttle System

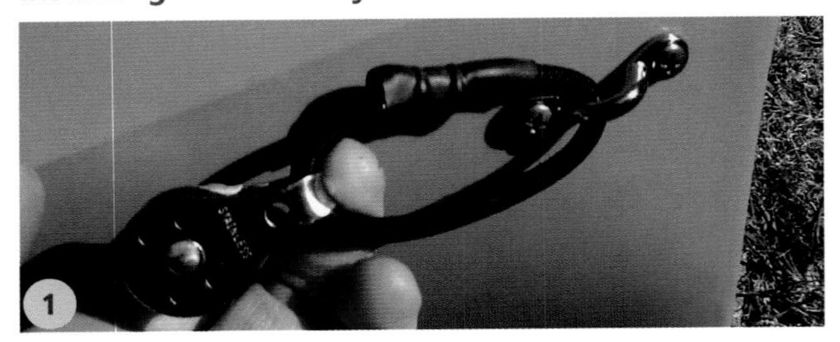

Use a loop of bungee at one end of your trolley to keep tension on the anchor shuttle.

Stainless hog rings like those used to construct crab pots are a great way to make connections with rope and bungee cord.

The stainless steel ring in conjunction with the carabiner allows the use of anchor lines and stake out poles.

Ladder cleats are great because they are multi-directional and allow quick release of the anchor line in a pinch.

If you use cut bait, a medium Tupperware® container is perfect. Prepare your bait well before your trip. I cut all my bait ahead of time and store it in a similar container with a re-freezable ice block. At the end of the day, if I still have bait, the whole thing goes in the freezer. If I use all my bait the container and ice block go into the dishwasher.

This angler has been fishing from his canoe for several years. Locally he is called the "Original Kayak Angler." He uses a double-bladed paddle to propel his craft.

The author's "old-school" crate setup from his early kayak fishing days, circa 1997.

Dry Bags and Boxes

Even though you think your kayak is dry inside, water can still find a way to ruin your cell phone or get your wallet wet. Dry bags and boxes come in virtually every shape and size. I suggest you at least get a small one to protect your cell phone and wallet. Experience has shown me that no kayak storage well is 100% waterproof.

Tackle Boxes

There are several types of tackle boxes to choose from depending on your preferences and needs. Keep in mind that you want to select a box that will store securely while you are paddling from place to place.

My favorite tackle boxes are the waterproof Plano® boxes. They have an o-ring and more latches to keep the saltwater from rusting your hooks. I do not put wet lures back in the box until I can rinse them in fresh water and then allow them to dry. Because fishing can vary from day to day, I pack three Plano® boxes with lures I know will catch fish, so their contents change with every trip.

Crate Systems and Coolers

Most kayak anglers are discovering the advantages of using a milk crate for on-kayak storage. The cool thing about using a milk crate is that its construction allows accessories, such as rod holders and pliers sheaths, to be attached to the crate. These are especially popular with the SOT crowd. A well-packed milk crate can turn any kayak into a floating tackle box. If you are not a "do it yourselfer" there are some nice commercially made kayak tackle storage systems available. Precision Pak® has a great system called the Yakmate. They come in two sizes and in three colors. One Yakmate style has a place for a stern light. These crates can also be used as a handy basket to carry your stuff to and from the kayak. Coolers are handy and many soft-sided coolers will fit inside most kayaks or in the tank wells. I like to keep my food and beverages cool on those hot summer days. I use two containers so my food and beverages do not end up tasting like bait.

Electronics

Power Sources

Before installing any electronics, consider what type of power source you want to use as well as voltage, weight, and space limitations. The power source should be water resistant, if not waterproof. Most electronics are powered by 12-volt systems. I have developed a system that fulfills the need of kayak anglers. It is compact, light, and waterproof. By using a cigarette plug, this battery can be used to power other items such as a cell phone charger. I use a trickle charger to maintain the batteries. Use two, keep the spare hooked up to the charger, and rotate them after every fishing trip. In the next section, I'll describe how to make it.

Building a Kayak Power Source

Step 1: Gather the materials needed (Figure 1):

- Dry box: Any size will do. I use the Extreme dry box that measures 10" x 5" x 5".
- Waterproof cigarette plug and receptacle: These are available at boating supply stores.
- 2-12 marine wire: This is the two-stranded 12-gauge wire used in boats.
- Female wiring connectors: These are the crimping type of connectors that connect to the battery and the back of the receptacle.

Step 2: Mark the area on the box where you plan to install the receptacle. On this box the plug must be at one end so that it will clear the battery on the inside. Cut out the hole and install the plug as described by its instructions. (Figure 2)

Step 3: Seal the backside of the plug with marine adhesive sealant and let dry. (Figure 3)

Step 4: Strip and solder the ends of the wires leaving extra room for positioning. (Figure 4)

Step 5: Crimp the female connectors onto each end of the 2-12 wire. (Figure 5)

Step 6: Connect the red (or yellow) wire to the positive (+) plug on the back of the receptacle. Plug the black wire onto the negative (-) plug. For protection, put an inline fuse on the positive side of the wire. (Figure 6)

Step 7: Connect the wires to the battery using the same wiring combination as above, red (or yellow) (+) and black (–). (Figure 7)

Step 8: Place the connected battery inside the box. My battery fits snugly so there is no need to add extra support. If your battery moves around in the box, add some foam to make it snug. Be sure not to allow anything to touch the contacts or interfere with the wiring. (Figure 8)

Step 9: Test the battery by plugging in the accessory you plan to use with it. (Figure 9)

Building a Power Source

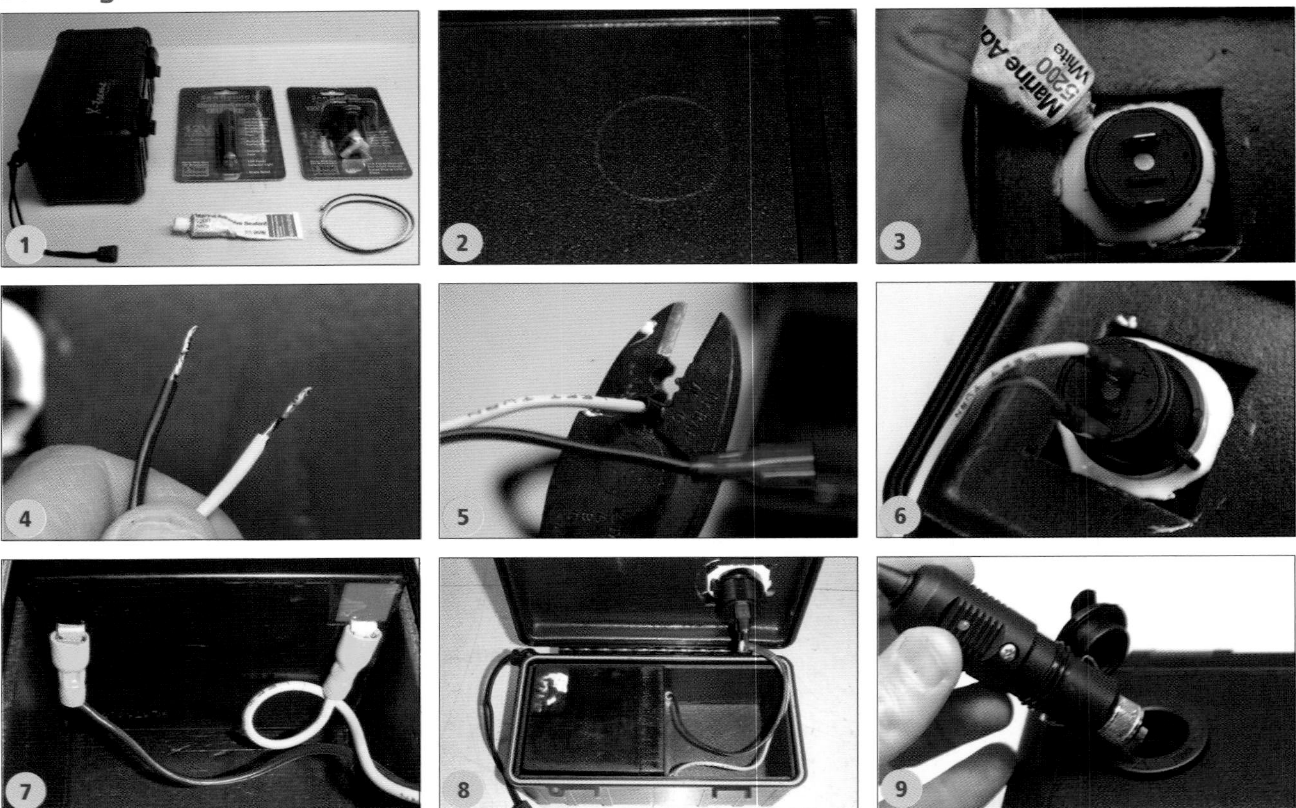

This setup separates the GPS from the depth finder allowing the angler to leave the kayak and still use the handheld GPS.

Fish Finders

Installing a Fish Finder

In this section I will describe, step by step, how to install a fish finder/depth sounder. Before you drill any holes or do any cutting, make sure to position the equipment so it will not get in your way while paddling. Get everything just right, before you commit to altering the hull of your kayak.

Materials needed:

- Fish finder: I suggest using the smaller, inexpensive units. A good system will cost around $100. Here we use the Eagle CUDA® 168 sounder. This unit is waterproof and should hold up to all the punishment you can give it.
- Foam block: This will be used as the support to help keep the transducer in place while the epoxy sets up. It will also protect the transducer from other things shifting around inside the kayak.
- 100 grit sandpaper: This is used to roughen the area where the transducer will be epoxied to the boat hull.
- Long set epoxy: The longer it takes to cure the better chance that there will be no air bubbles under the transducer after curing. Here we used Evercoat® Marine Resin, it typically takes about 30 minutes to set up.
- Lexel® Adhesive: This is used to glue the foam block down to the inside of the hull. It is also used to seal areas where brackets are attached or where holes are drilled into the hull.
- Cable ties or Velcro® straps: There will be an excess of cable. Use these to get the wires out of the way.

Installing a Fish Finder

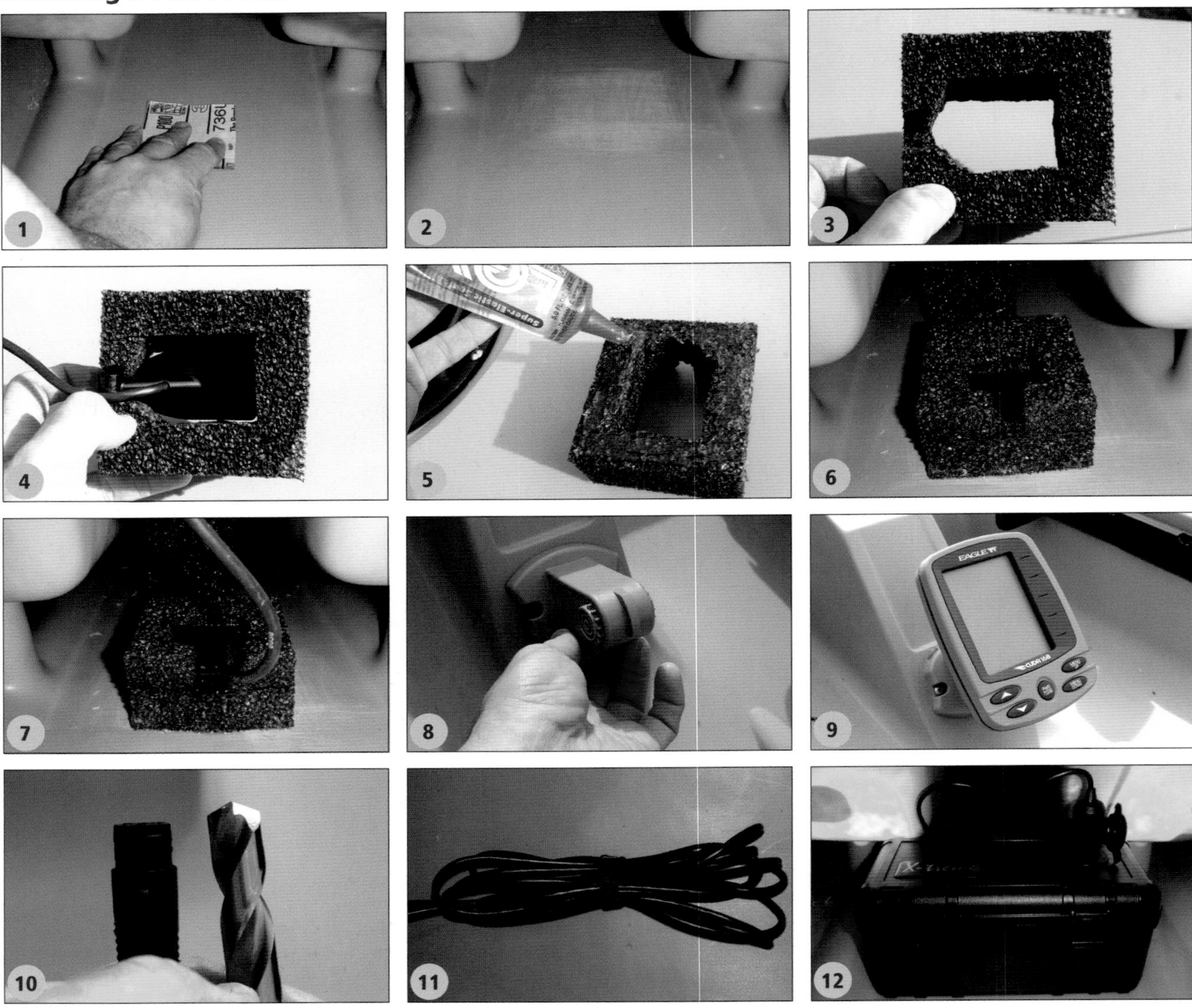

Installing the Transducer

I prefer using epoxy rather than rubber and plastic adhesives. Epoxy sets hard and allows a solid signal to penetrate the hull. This is a shoot-through-the-hull design so temperature sensors will not be as accurate, however the sonar signal should not be affected. Because we are using slow-set epoxy this is a 2-day project. Be patient and do not rush and you will have an application that will last as long as your kayak.

Step 1. Use 100 grit sandpaper to roughen up the area where you intend to epoxy your transducer. (Figure 1) Sand an area about twice as big as you need to ensure good adhesion.

Step 2. There should be no gloss left in the area you sand. The rougher the plastic the better it will hold. (Figure 2) Clean the area thoroughly with denatured alcohol.

Step 3. Take your foam block and cut out an area big enough to hold the transducer. An easy way to do this is to trace the shape of your transducer on the block and cut it out. (Figure 3) This should go all the way through, with at least an half of an inch of foam left to surround the transducer.

Step 4. The transducer should drop through the block as it must allow the epoxy and bubbles to flow up and around the transducer. (Figure 4) Trim the bottom of the block to fit the contour of your kayak. Most SOT kayaks have a flat bottom so you will not need to trim the block. If the hull has an angle, trim the foam block to fit.

Step 5. Coat the bottom of the block with the marine adhesive and place it firmly on the sanded area. (Figure 5) It is a good idea to weight the block down. A brick will work just fine. Now let this set up according to the adhesive's directions.

Step 6. Make sure that there are no gaps between the foam and the floor of the kayak. If there is a gap, fill it with the marine adhesive. This is important because if it is not sealed the epoxy will seep out and the transducer will not work. Now that the block is sealed pour enough slow-set epoxy to fill the block about a third of the way. (Figure 6) Push the transducer down into the block until it hits the bottom, epoxy will push up and around the transducer so wear some gloves. Use a weight to hold the transducer to the bottom of the block until the epoxy cures. I use slow-set epoxy (30-minutes to 1-hour cure time), this way no bubbles get set in the epoxy.

Step 7. When the first pour sets I add more epoxy to completely cover the transducer. (Figure 7) After the second application sets, you have successfully installed the transducer. If you want a less permanent application, use Lexel® sealant instead of epoxy. It will allow removal of the transducer, but it is more prone to create air bubbles.

Installing the Display Unit

Step 8. Before drilling any holes sit in the kayak and locate a good place for the display. It should not be in the way of your paddle stroke, but close enough to control the functions of the unit. On most SOT kayaks, the best place is the console area between the foot wells. (Figure 8) The good thing about the smaller units is that they can be mounted with their supplied brackets. This allows the unit to be removed to prevent theft.

Step 9. Once you find your kayak's sweet spot, cover the bottom of the bracket with Lexel® and attach it to the kayak using stainless steel hardware. (Figure 9)

Step 10. Now is the most painful part, drilling the holes for the wires to connect to the display unit. Try to make the holes for the wires as small as possible. (Figure 10) Most units will come with a cover for this hole. After positioning the wires, fill the hole with marine adhesive and use the supplied cover. When this application sets, apply more adhesive to the inside. If done correctly, the application will be completely waterproof.

Step 11. Connect the cables to the display and you are almost done. Use the Velcro straps to secure excess wires out of the way. Do not shorten or cut the transducer cable, because splices will affect the signal integrity. (Figure 11)

Installing the Battery

Step 12. Just about any battery combination that provides 12 volts of power can be used to supply power to the depth finder. I use the power source and waterproof plug described in the previous section. Connect the waterproof cigarette lighter plug to the fish finder's power cable and connect it to the power supply. (Figure 12)

Go test your unit. If installed correctly, you should have no problems. If there is a problem, first check all connections. If there is a signal problem you may have to reinstall the transducer.

Front and rear views of a Wilderness Systems Tarpon 140 kayak rigged for fly fishing.

Rigged for fly fishing at the Chesapeake Bay Bridge Tunnel. The front rod holder is removable for casting.

Three kayaks ready for a surf launch in Virginia Beach. The angler in the background is waiting for signs of feeding fish.

A Native Watercraft Ultimate 14.5 ready for a fall spotted trout run in Virginia Beach.

Seasonal Kayak Fishing

Two-piece dry top/pants combinations are an effective way to protect you from the elements and immersion. Wearing a correctly fitting PFD is the key to making this work.

Most folks prefer to kayak fish when the weather is perfect. The fact is, that if you go by that mentality you will not get a lot of time on the water. With the right clothing and gear, you can kayak fish safely and comfortably year-round. Here in Virginia we have a variety of seasons from hot and humid summers, to cold and windy winters. So, I need a variety of protective clothing and measures. The following section breaks the seasons down into Fall/Winter and Spring/Summer. Granted these seasons may vary where you live, but the key is to prevent exposure, whether hot or cold.

Fall and Winter

Cold weather paddling is probably the most risky of all aspects of the sport. But, with proper attire, you can make the experience quite comfortable, safe, and fun. We have a saying "dress for the water." The object is to minimize exposure to both cold air and water (if you go in). When you are exposed to very cold water the reflex is to inhale. When this happens you can take water into your lungs. Surprisingly, that is what causes most cold-water drowning. Proper attire can limit exposure to cold water and even eliminate this reflex. It can also prevent hypothermia and buy enough time to get back onto your kayak or until help arrives. Hypothermia occurs when your body temperature goes so low that necessary functions, such as breathing and circulation, either slow or stop. Hypothermia can occur in water temps as high as 80°F. In water, the body cools 25% quicker than in air. The water temperature, your physical attributes, and movement all have an effect on how long it takes hypothermia to set in. See the chart below for more information.

Even though it is cold, you must also consider sun and wind protection for your face. Sunscreen and lip protection are good ideas in colder climates. It is just as important to drink water in the winter as it is in the summer, so stay hydrated. Don't forget to bring along your polarized sunglasses. Here are a few options for cold water paddling attire.

Head Gear

Because most heat loss occurs from the head a good warm hat is necessary. Materials vary from wool to polypropylene. All are an effective way to keep your head and ears warm. Fleece skull caps are nice. They have little bulk and some have waterproof linings. They work even when wet. Another option is a neoprene hood, like scuba divers wear. However, I find they affect my hearing.

Dry Suits

A dry suit is the most effective way to prevent exposure and is also the most expensive, especially breathable types. Dry suits offer protection both in and out of the water. They are totally sealed at the neck, arms, and legs. They are a little harder to get into, and unless they have a "relief zipper" can be hard to get out of when "nature calls." By layering with fleece you have a combination that can handle the coldest of waters. If you plan on spending a lot of time kayak fishing in cold climates, then a dry suit should be your first choice of paddling apparel. Don't forget to wear your PFD. Just because you are dry doesn't mean that you can't drown. Dry suits

Here is the author wearing an NRS exteme relief dry suit preparing for a winter fishing trip. Photo by Wayne Bradby.

Water Temp. (degrees F)	Exhaustion or Hypothermia	Survival Time
32.5	under 15 minutes	under 15 to 45 minutes
32.5 to 40	15 to 30 minutes	30 to 90 minutes
40 to 50	30 to 60 minutes	1 to 3 hours
50 to 60	1 to 2 hours	1 to 6 hours
60 to 70	2 to 7 hours	2 to 40 hours
70 to 80	2 to 12 hours	3 hours to indefinite
over 80	indefinite	indefinite

Information courtesy of the United States Coast Guard.

are a good idea when fishing open ocean waters. I prefer the "dry" suits to "wet" suits because I am not exposed to the water. See the wet suit section for further information on its effectiveness.

Dry Top and Pants

This combination is a little more specific to the sport of kayaking. Dry pants or bibs are much like breathable waders, except they have a rubber gasket that seals the pants at the ankle. Dry tops are also sealed at the wrists and at the neck. Most dry tops are also designed to form a water tight seal when used with the dry pants. These outfits are usually made from Gore-tex® or other waterproof breathable material. Combine with a layer of fleece, and neoprene booties, and you have an effective barrier against the elements. It is a good idea to reinforce this combination by wearing a snug PFD. If you go over you might get some water but not enough that you will not be able to get back on your kayak.

Wayne Bradby donning his dry top and wader outfit—a very popular combination with kayak anglers.

Waders

Most kayak anglers were once shore anglers. Many times shore anglers have seen kayak anglers catching fish just beyond the reach of their cast. So they go out and buy a kayak. Every shore angler has at least one pair of waders. Waders are good for kayak angling, keeping you dry and warm. These are especially useful for Sit On Top kayaks, where paddle drip and water in the foot wells can get you wet. Neoprene waders are preferred over vinyl and rubber versions. If you go over board, they won't drown you. Neoprene is buoyant. Its tight fit will allow little water to intrude and your body heat will warm this small amount of water. A layer of fleece will help keep you warm, even if you get wet. A wading belt should always be worn to help minimize the amount of water that gets into the waders. I prefer breathable waders as they allow perspiration to escape and with a layer of Capilene® or other synthetic (hydrophobic) fleece. They are just as warm as neoprene but less bulky and not as heavy. By layering a waterproof jacket, or paddle top, under your PFD you will have an effective system for kayak fishing. This system is good for all conditions, but I prefer to use it when I am going wading.

Wet Suits

This option is not the route that I would take. Wet suits work by allowing a layer of water inside to keep you warm. It will keep you warm if you're sitting on a kayak but, if you go over, water will enter the wet suit. At first it will be cold and may cause cold-water shock. In a short time, your body will warm the water and you will become comfortable. Once out of the water, the warm water layer drains and the wet suit cools down. This can be uncomfortable. Unlike neoprene waders, which keep you dry, wet suits are not designed for use out of the water.

Summary

Even though you are protected from the elements it is still a good idea to practice capsizing your kayak and self-rescues. Check your local paddle shop or outfitter for details. I can tell you from experience it is good to know what to do when trouble happens.

I hope you enjoyed this information and that these suggestions will help extend your fishing seasons. Be smart and safe, and always wear your PFD.

Spring and Summer

Spring is in the air! As air and water temperatures begin to climb, it is time to put away the dry suit and get out the sunscreen.

Sun Protection

This brings me to the most important item in your warm-weather kayaking arsenal, sun protection. Now that we understand the danger of skin cancer is very real, it is best to take the maximum precaution to prevent overexposure. Before going outside, I slather on my favorite sunscreen. I use a non-greasy hypoallergenic 25-30 rated SPF and really make sure to get areas that get the most exposure, like my neck, face, ears, arms, and the backs of my hands. For additional protection, I wear long-sleeved shirts and zip-off pants that are made of quick drying SPF-rated material. Look for polyester and cotton blends, these won't feel like you are wearing garbage bags. For further protection, I wear a wide-brimmed boonie hat and an angler Buff®. In extreme cases, a pair of sun gloves protects the backs of my hands. If you become overheated, find some shallow water and go for a dip or splash some water on yourself to cool off. Don't forget your PFD. There are models that use mesh in their construction to keep you cooler, and remember, it won't do you any good if you aren't wearing it.

Wading Shoes

Because I wade, I protect my feet with a pair of wading shoes. I prefer dive booties, or true wading shoes to sandals. An old pair of tennis shoes will also work. The open areas in sandals will not fully

In warmer seasons, combine a dry top or wading jacket with a pair of waders. This system is great for wading in conditions where the water is too cold to wet wade.

The author takes sun protection very seriously, even though it may look silly. Photo by Mark Lozier.

protect you from shells or crab pinches. They also let in the sun and give you that funky tiger-striped foot tan. Wading booties are easy to remove and to swim with if you decide to take a dip.

Apparel

Wearing quick-dry long pants will protect you from jellyfish and hydroid stings. I bring along a pair of breathable waders and a breathable wading jacket to protect me from the morning chill. They make good rain gear if the weather suddenly turns nasty.

Water

On a side note, it is a good idea to bring lots of water and stay hydrated. I fill two 32-oz Nalgene bottles with about 30 oz and freeze them. This is my primary water supply. I also freeze six small 12-oz plastic bottles and put them in my soft-sided cooler to keep my lunch cool. Throughout the day they melt and become a refreshing drink. This is a good way to ensure you drink water all day, "as it melts, drink a little." Be sure to eat to keep up your energy level.

Safety

Because warmer temperatures harbor unstable weather patterns, it is a good idea to listen to the NOAA weather forecasts and alerts. Most marine VHF radios have this feature and automatically broadcast the weather alerts for your area. Keep an eye on the sky for thunderheads or anvil-shaped clouds, and if you hear thunder, you are in range of a lightning strike. If you get caught in open water during a storm, get as low as possible on your kayak and lay all your fishing rods down. Get to safety as soon as possible. A bridge makes a nice place to weather out a thunderstorm. Otherwise head for shore, being careful not to get broadsided by waves.

The author's Redfish 14 at Jamaica Bay, New York City.

Transporting Your Kayak

Properly strapping down kayaks is very important, especially when traveling long distances. Photo courtesy of Chad Hoover.

Car Topping

One of the best attributes of a kayak is its portability. However, when transporting kayaks on vehicles it is best to use extreme caution and to use proven equipment. The best systems are those made especially for your vehicle, such as those by Yakima and Thule. These systems are designed to use the vehicle's structural design and/or factory racks. If they are installed correctly they are indestructible.

I highly recommend that if you go with one of these systems, take advantage of professional installation by factory-certified technicians. Most outfitters selling these brands have a trained technician on staff. Once the base and bars are installed, there are a plethora of saddles that make attaching a kayak a breeze. Soft kayak racks that use straps and foam pads are okay for short trips but, if you have the budget, get a fixed system.

Once you have a rack system installed, how do you get the kayak up there? Well, the best solution is to have two folks lift the kayak onto the saddles. The best way for a one-person job is to use a loader bar. Yakima makes an extender that slides out of the crossbar. This extension allows you to lift the bow of the kayak to the racks. You can then lift the stern onto the saddles. It is a very simple solution and makes loading a breeze. I own a Chevy Avalanche and have it set up with the Yakima bars attached to the factory-installed rails. I use Yakima Mako saddles to hold the kayak, Fatcat 4 to hold rods, and multi-mounts to carry paddles and push poles. Combine them with the Boatlocker and you have a secure way to keep everything ready for your next trip. Using the truck bed to load and unload my kayak, allows me to simply slide it onto the saddles from the back.

Most systems come with straps to secure the kayak to the saddles. These are very effective if connected using the manufacturer's instructions. Bow and stern straps should be added as well. They will hold the kayak in place and act as a safety in case the main straps fail. In an accident, you want the kayak to stay attached to the vehicle. A detached kayak may cause damage or injury to other drivers.

Security is a big concern for kayak anglers. Cable locks are a great way to keep honest folks honest.

The best way to carry kayaks is on a system made to work with your vehicle's factory racks. Companies like Yakima and Thule make racks that are specific to vehicle makes and models. Be sure to follow the manufacturers' instructions.

Truck Beds

Truck beds are handy. They allow you to carry fully rigged kayaks upright. The catch is that most truck beds are 6 to 8 feet long and most kayaks are 10 to 16 feet long. 10-foot kayaks are fine in 8-foot beds but the longer kayaks will hang over too much. The solution is to use a bed extender. The extender plugs into the hitch receiver and creates a support for the extra length. Be sure to check your local laws.

Bed extenders are necessary if you are hauling kayaks that extend beyond the tailgate. Don't forget to put an orange flag on the stern of these kayaks.

Most states require a flag on objects that extend out from vehicles. Securely strap your kayaks in the truck bed using the scupper holes, which make excellent attachment points for straps. Simply thread the straps or ropes through the holes.

Trailers

Trailers are becoming more popular for kayak anglers, especially when carrying multiple kayaks. Trailers are available for carrying any number of kayaks and can transport them fully rigged. Most trailers are lower to the ground and you won't have to lift the kayak over your head. However, you will need to find launch areas that have trailer parking and you will need trailer storage. I use my trailer as a portable storage rack. It keeps my kayaks up off the ground and can be ready to go in a moment's notice. If storing kayaks on a trailer, make sure to use a hull-friendly saddle system. Also use a support system to get the weight off the leaf springs while the trailer sits. It is a good idea to keep the bearings lubricated and check their wear once a year. I use Bearing Buddy® to keep my hubs lubricated and clean.

This truck is equipped with overhead racks and a bed extender.

Road-ready kayak trailers are available from companies like Trailex (shown here) and Rack-n-Roll.

A kayak trailer ready for a tournament trip from Virginia to Florida.

A homemade trailer using a wooden frame on a folding trailer. If you make a trailer have it checked by a state DOT official before hitting the road.

Kayak Storage

Properly storing a kayak can make it last a lifetime. A cool area indoors is the best place to store a kayak. Ideally, an air-conditioned garage is the ticket but a crawlspace or basement will work as good, as long as it is cool. Hot storage buildings will soften the hull and cause deformity. Outdoor storage is okay as long as the kayak is out of direct sunlight. I store my kayaks in shaded racks behind my house. They handle it well and look as good as new. A tarp will create shade and keep out harmful UV rays. If the inside is dry, close all hatches to prevent any stowaways. A SINK will need a cockpit cover.

Sunsets like this make even a slow day of fishing "picture perfect."

Let's Go Fishing

Mark Lozier, guide for Ruthless Fishing, with a nice redfish.

Kayak Positioning and Maneuvering

Basic Paddle Strokes

All kayak anglers should strive to learn the following basic paddle skills. This is just an overview and is in no way a substitute for taking a class with a certified ACA instructor.

Forward Stroke

The forward stroke is the basic stroke used to propel your kayak forward. This stroke gets you to and from your favorite fishing hole. Learning the proper technique will make you a more efficient and controlled paddler. If you have a problem paddling in a straight line, it is likely your paddle stroke and not the kayak. Most paddlers paddle incorrectly because they are using their arms rather than their upper body. A proper forward stroke uses upper body strength and proper arm extension. A good sign of efficient paddling is silent paddling, if you hear the paddle splashing, then you are not paddling efficiently. Here are the basic steps for a forward stroke.

1. The first maneuver is called the *catch*. Place the paddle blade into the water near your feet. Try to create as little splash as possible and keep the paddle close to the kayak.
2. The second maneuver is the *pull*. Starting at your feet, turn your body at the waist while pulling the paddle so the water moves parallel to the kayak. As you are pulling the paddle with one arm, balance the other arm with constant pressure. You are not actually pushing the paddle with the opposite arm, just holding it. Stop when the paddle blade is just behind your hips. Reaching too far back or forward with your paddle will cause the kayak to turn and affect the course.
3. The third and final maneuver is the *lift*. Pull the paddle up and out of the water. The blade should cut through the water with no resistance at all. Now place the opposite blade into the water at your feet and repeat.

Reverse Stroke

The reverse stroke is just like the forward stroke, only backwards. The steps are the same, but the key of the reverse stroke is to always look to see where you are heading.

Sweep Strokes

Use sweep strokes in both stationary and moving maneuvers. They can rotate the stationary kayak on its axis or be used while moving to initiate an

Forward Stroke

Catch: Place the paddle blade into the water near your feet without splashing. Keep the paddle close to the kayak.

Pull: Starting at your feet, turn your body at the waist while pulling the paddle so the water moves parallel to the kayak.

Lift: Pull the paddle up and out of the water. The blade should cut through the water with no resistance at all.

Reverse Stroke

Catch: Place the paddle blade into the water behind you, without splashing. Keep the paddle close to the kayak.

Pull: Turn your body at the waist while pulling the paddle forward so the water moves parallel to the kayak.

Lift: Pull the paddle up and out of the water. The blade should cut through the water with no resistance at all.

Sweep Strokes

Place the blade into the water at your feet with your arm fully extended. Place opposite arm in comfortable position lower than your shoulder.

Twist your torso so the paddle travels in a wide arc.

Keeping your eyes on the paddle, continue to rotate until your paddle is almost touching the kayak behind you.

immediate turn. After the basic sweep techniques are mastered you can add a technique called *edging* to make the turn even more efficient. This is simply leaning the kayak into the direction you want to turn. Here are the basic steps.

1. Place the blade into the water at your feet, as in the forward stroke, but with your arm fully extended. During the stroke your arm should always be extended. Your opposite arm should be in the most comfortable position and kept lower than your shoulder.
2. Twist your torso so the paddle travels in a wide arc.
3. Keeping your eyes on the paddle, continue to rotate until your paddle is almost touching the kayak behind you. Remember to keep your arm extended. Repeat until you are facing the intended direction.

The sweep technique can be reversed by combining a forward sweep on one side and a reverse sweep on the other. You can rotate the kayak in a stationary position using this combination. It is handy for maneuvering the kayak while drifting through a fishing hole. Basically, it makes your turn more efficient by using the curvature of the hull. It is not a difficult technique, although you are more likely to turtle.

Place the paddle blade in the water about a foot from the kayak. Keep the paddle at a high angle and the blade close to the kayak.

Use a figure-8 motion with long strokes to move the the kayak sideways.

Pressing in towards the kayak, keep the motion slow and smooth with no splashes. The kayak will slowly move to the side.

Draw Strokes

Draw strokes are used to maneuver the kayak laterally. This stroke allows you to move the kayak sideways without unnecessary kayak maneuvers. It is a useful maneuver when fishing around pilings or in areas where turning space is limited. I use this maneuver a lot to set up over structures. There are a few types of draw strokes. The most efficient and stealthy is the sculling draw. Here is how to do it.

1. Place the paddle blade in the water about a foot from the kayak. Keep the paddle at a high angle and the paddle blade close to the kayak.

2. Think about spreading peanut butter on a piece of bread. Using a figure-8 motion, spread the peanut butter beside the kayak. Longer strokes work best. Short sloppy strokes are inefficient.

3. Keeping the pressure towards your kayak, the motion should be slow and smooth with no splashes. The kayak will slowly and smoothly move to the side.

Braking and Bracing

Braking is used to stop the forward motion of the kayak and is basically a modified reverse stroke. You use the paddle to stop the kayak. When you want to stop, reach back with the paddle blade and dig it into the water. This is a good way to turn. If you keep the paddle there, you'll turn into the side that the paddle is on. To stop, simply alternate sides until you stop. If done effectively, you should be able to completely stop in the length of the kayak.

Bracing is used to prevent the kayak from overturning. By using the paddle to create resistance to the water surface, you can create enough force to counter capsizing. The key to bracing is timing. If you anticipate a capsize think quickly to effectively brace. This takes practice, but can become a lifesaver.

Maneuvering

One Hand Paddling

To effectively maneuver the kayak while fishing, have one hand on the paddle and the other on your fishing rod. I have found that the best way to one-arm paddle is to use your forearm as a brace. This will require some flexibility in your wrist, but the more you do it the easier it will get.

Braking

Braking allows you to stop the kayak in its own length. Reach back for maximum efficiency.

Before the kayak starts to turn, switch sides and make sure to reach back again.

Switch sides again and you should come to a complete stop.

One hand paddling allows you to maneuver your kayak while keeping a rod at the ready. Photo by Mark Lozier.

Native's Ultimate series of kayaks are excellent kayaks for standing, combined with the Watertrail paddle pole and you have a sight anglers dream. Photo by Mark Lozier.

Here the author uses his paddle to pole his kayak across a shallow flat. Photo by Matt Routh.

Poling Kayaks

Another way to maneuver a kayak is poling. This technique allows you to stand, which in turn gets you higher where it is easier to spot fish. Not all kayaks are suited to do this and neither are all kayakers. Some of the wider more stable kayaks, such as the Heritage Redfish or the Wilderness Systems Ride 135, are well suited for standing and poling. Grasping your paddle at one end makes an effective push pole in water up to a foot deep.

Drifting

Drifting is my favorite technique. It uses very little energy and is a great way to cover water and fish at the same time. In tidal areas, such as Lynnhaven Inlet, I can just about drift the whole time by using the tide cycle. I launch during the incoming tide, drift to my honey holes, fish that area at flood, fish the ebb, and then drift home on the outgoing tide. This only works in areas with tidal flow and takes some planning, but works very well. In certain conditions, drifting can be facilitated by rudders, drag anchors and drift chutes.

Using Drag Anchors and Drift Chutes

Drag anchors are used to slow the drift of a kayak. Consisting of a weight designed to drag across the bottom it creates enough resistance to slow down a drift. This method is used mostly on rivers that have bottoms with small rocks and debris. It does have a tendency to snag and cause problems.

Drift chutes are also called sea anchors. They are basically an underwater parachute that slows the drift, particularly in windy conditions, and are designed for use in open water. Unless you want to drift with the tide, they are not ideal in areas with lots of current. Drift chutes in the 12- to18-inch range are ideal for kayak fishing.

Using Rudders and Skegs

Rudders are mechanisms that allow the kayak to be steered using movable foot pedals. There are varying opinions on rudders and some advantages. Although substantially increasing the cost of kayaks, they do help keep the boat tracking straight in quartering seas and winds and maintain the desired direction while drifting. Simply use the rudder to steer the kayak in your desired direction. Good paddling technique can also perform these functions. If you can afford a rudder, then go for it. Otherwise you will probably not miss it. Proper paddle strokes are an excellent substitute for rudders.

Skegs are fixed control surfaces that are either molded into the hull or retractable. They do not facilitate steering, but help keep the kayak on track. The Native Ultimate 12 comes with a retractable skeg.

Anchoring

The easiest way to stay on a hot spot is to anchor. In some cases an anchor can be dangerous. I highly recommend only anchoring if the conditions are safe. Use extreme caution in areas with exceptionally fast currents. Do not anchor in these places and use alternate means to hold position. Many have learned that just tying an anchor to the side of your kayak can lead to disaster. So kayak anglers have developed a way to anchor that is more effective and less dangerous. This system utilizes a shuttle system that is not unlike the pulley clotheslines often seen between buildings. This system allows the anchor to be placed inline with the kayak, so there is less chance of capsizing. It also allows for quick disconnection in case of emergencies or to fight a fish.

Using the Stake Out Pole

The best way to anchor in shallow water is to use a stake out pole. Basically a stick or rod that is stuck into areas with soft substrates, a stake out pole can be made of an old broom handle or bought from suppliers such as Capt. Dick Enterprises. The Capt. Dick StakeOutPole™ is made of four-foot fiberglass with a machined aluminum tip at the bottom. The top has a foam grip and a lanyard attached. It pierces soft bottoms easily and even floats. When you reach an area you want to fish simply stick it in the bottom and attach it to the kayak or the shuttle system, then adjust the shuttle to get the correct angle and start casting. The Watertrail paddle pole can also be used as a stake out pole.

The Capt. Dick StakeOutPole™ is an effective way to anchor in skinny water with soft bottoms. Photo by Wayne Bradby.

Using the Anchor Shuttle System

This will work with all anchor types. Deploy the anchor as usual, when it holds, snap the rope into the carabiner. Make sure the rope can flow through the ring. Using the pulleys, move the carabiner to the front or to the rear of the kayak. When it gets there, attach the rope to the cleat. The kayak will position itself inline with the anchor. Let out additional line if you need to. You can also use the anchor shuttle with the stake out pole and with drift anchors. The shuttle system will also allow you to adjust the angle of your kayak in relationship to the current. (See illustrations on following page.) To retrieve the anchor, remove the line from the cleat and pull it in while the carabiner is at the end. This will use the length of the boat to retrieve the anchor. When the anchor reaches the surface pull it to the center using the shuttle line and take the line out of the carabiner. If things ever go wrong, dump the anchor with the attached float and get it later when conditions are safer.

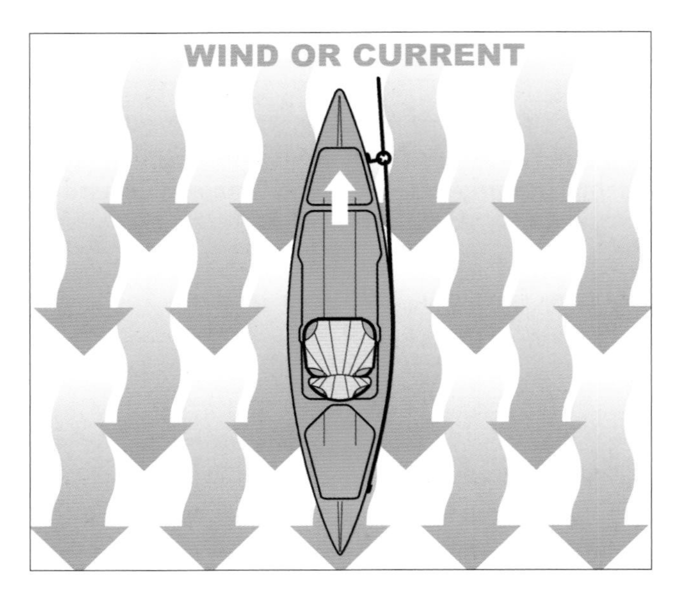

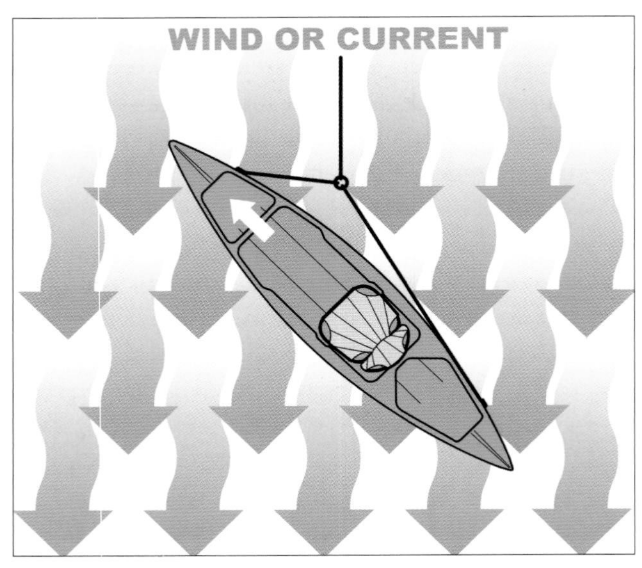

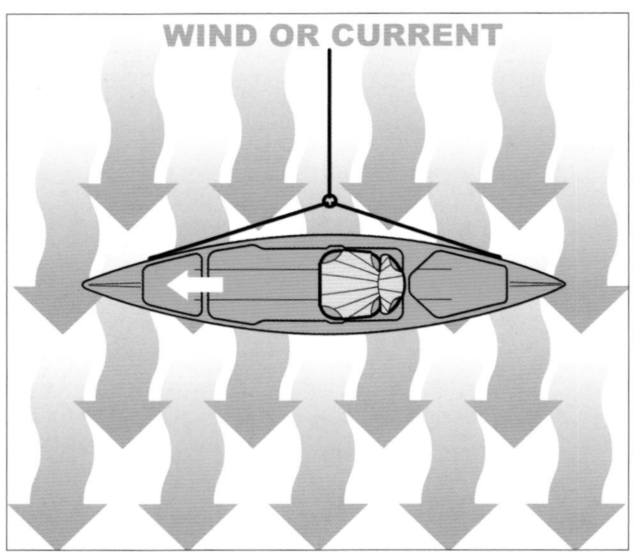

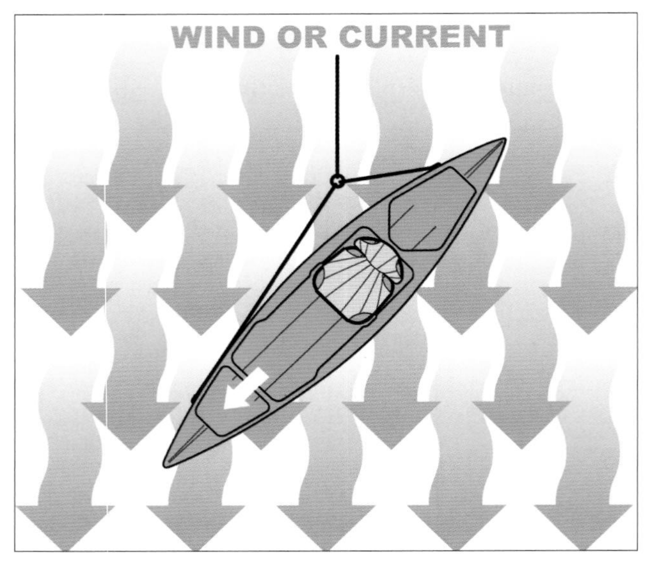

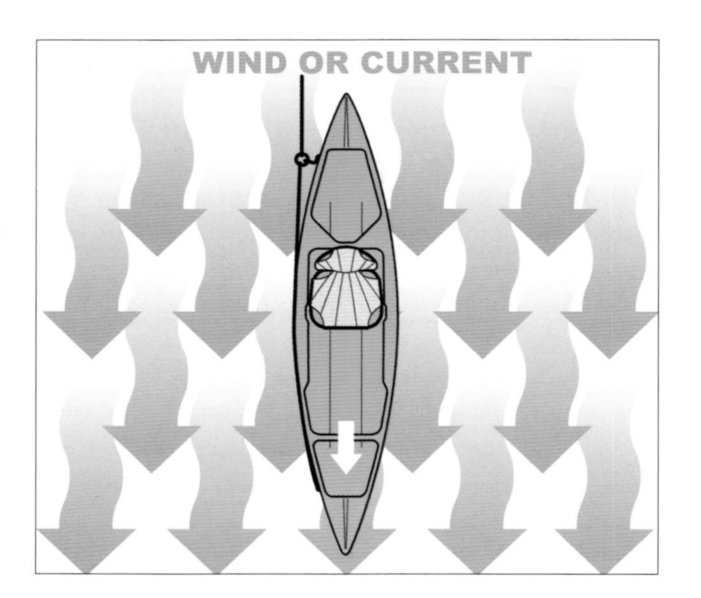

These pictures show how different positions of the anchor shuttle affect the direction the kayak faces. Illustrations courtesy of Native Watercraft.

Wedging

Wedging is a term coined by fellow freshwater kayak angler Jeff Little. I have been using this technique for some time, but did not have a good term for it. Thanks Jeff!

Wedging is using some sort of natural structure to hold the kayak in position. Whether you use a shoal, bank, rock, or grass island. In essence, beaching your kayak on this structure to hold it in position. Jeff prefers this to using an anchor on flowing rivers. He simply wedges the kayak on structure in the river. Just be careful not to get stuck. In the marsh, I back the kayak into the grass so that it is held in place. This is a very stealthy approach and great for staking out a honey hole.

Trolling

Trolling is a very popular way to fish from a kayak, especially from pedal-powered kayaks such as the Hobie MirageDrive kayaks. It is the most efficient way to maximize your time on the water. Trolling is nothing more that towing the lure or bait behind the kayak. The Scotty rod holders were originally meant for this purpose—they allow the rod angle and direction to be adjusted so that they are out of the way of your paddle stroke. The rod can be placed either behind or in front of the angler, but most anglers prefer their rod up front where they can keep an eye on it. It is also a lot easier to grab the fishing rod if it is in front of you. Trolling requires that the kayak be in constant motion, so it can be a very physical way of fishing. There are several ways to get your lures/bait to the desired depth. The most common way is to buy weighted or lipped lures that dive to given depths. Inline weights, downriggers, and planers can also be used to get the lures to the desired depth.

Side Saddle

One of the most commonly used kayak fishing positions is side saddle. This is most handy on the flats where you can touch bottom while sitting on the kayak. Having both feet on the bottom will allow you to control the kayak direction. This works well with mild currents and in windy conditions. I like to compare it to walking with your feet while sitting in a wheelchair. You can control the position and the direction of the kayak, and if you want to drift, simply pick up your feet and float to the next spot. Sitting side saddle is also a good way to fight fish, as it puts the fish broadside to the kayak.

Sitting side saddle is a great way to control the kayak, and a great way to fish fish from a kayak.

Preparing for a Kayak Fishing Trip

Quality rods and reels can make the trip. The author uses rods by St. Croix and reels by Shimano.

Fishing Rods and Reels

Choosing rods and reels can be almost as confusing as choosing a kayak. It can really go beyond the scope of this book. Basically, you want a rod long enough to work around your kayak, powerful enough to handle the fish you are pursuing, and matched to the line, reel, and terminal tackle you are using. If you are an avid angler, you may already have the equipment you need. New anglers will need to pick the right equipment. Rod and reel selection can be very subjective, but the general choice among kayak anglers is a rod in the 6 to 7 foot range. This length of fishing rod can be found in just about every action and power available. The key is to balance the rod, reel, and line. Before you buy, look at the specs and try and balance your outfit. You do not want to put a 20-pound class reel on a 2-pound class rod. Your local tackle shop should be able to set you up with a balanced outfit.

The power of a rod refers to how much force it takes to flex. Rod powers are engineered to handle a certain range of lure weights and lines. Selecting a rod power is as simple as finding the rod that is designed to cast the weight of the terminal tackle you most commonly use. Power is classified as UL (ultra light), L (light), ML (medium light), M (medium), MH (medium heavy), H (heavy), and XH (extra heavy). The action of a rod is determined by where a rod flexes along the blank. Faster action rods flex mostly near the tip, moderate action rods flex near the middle, and slower rods flex down into the butt section. Most rods are classified as XF (extra fast), F (fast), MF (moderate fast), M (moderate) and S (slow).

Most rod manufacturers will give the power and action in the model name. For example, the St. Croix Rod Company abbreviates the following information: model name, rod type, length in feet and inches, power, and action. So the AVS60LF model is an Avid Series (AV), spinning (S), 6'0" long, light (L) power, fast (F) action rod.

Spinning vs. Casting

I get a lot of questions on the advantages of spinning reels over casting reels. This preference is very subjective, but I'll tell you my take on these reel types. Spinning tackle is more forgiving and will usually cast lighter lures farther than casting gear. Spinning tackle is ideal for beginners or for casting in windy conditions. The disadvantage is that the spinning gear creates line twist and may cause tangles. Casting reels also take a little more attention. First you need to make sure the reel is properly adjusted for the lure weight you are using. There are several ways to adjust this and it varies from reel to reel. You must learn to thumb the reel. This allows you put tension on the spool during the cast and to stop the lure by stopping the spool, which lets you accurately place a lure at the desired distance. Casting reels have almost no line twist, and with a braided line have more capacity than comparable spinning reels. The main disadvantage is backlash. Even seasoned pros like me will blow a cast and backlash the reel. A backlashed reel can take a long time to untangle. That is why I always carry two rod and reel combos.

Because I fish both fresh and saltwater, I own a wide range of rods and reels. Here are the combinations that I commonly use and the situations that I use them in. All the rods discussed are by St. Croix and the reels manufactured by Shimano.

Nothing can slow down fishing more than a backlashed reel.

Spinning

Avid Model #AVS60LF

This is the lightest rod I use on a kayak. This 6-foot rod is rated for 4 to 8-pound test and will cast lures in the 1⁄16–1⁄4 ounce range. I use a Sahara 1500 spooled with 15-pound test Powerpro (4-pound mono diameter). This rod is best suited for casting weedless jerk shads or small crappie jigs. I use this rod for lighter presentations in shallow salt and freshwater.

Avid Model #AVS60MF

This 6-foot rod is rated for 6 to12-pound test, the lure weight is 3⁄16–5⁄8 ounces. This rod gets a Sahara 2500 reel spooled with 20-pound test Powerpro (6-pound mono diameter). It fits the same presentation type as the previous rod but is used for slightly larger jigs and lures.

These six rods cover all the saltwater species that the author prefers to fish. They range from 6 to 30-pound line classes.

These are the two rods I give clients when fishing local tidal flats. They work well on the 12-foot kayaks I typically use on charters.

Legend Inshore Model #LIS70LM
This 7-foot rod is rated for 6 to 12-pound test lines and lure weight of ⅛–⅜ ounces. This rod is equipped with a Stradic 2500 spooled with 20-pound test Powerpro (6-pound mono diameter). This is my light presentation rod when it is windy. I use it for casting weedless plastics, light jigs, and crankbaits in both fresh and saltwater.

Legend Inshore Model #LIS70MHF
This 7-foot rod is rated for 10 to 20-pound test, and lures in the ½ to 1¼ ounces range. I use a Stradic 4000 reel spooled with 50-pound test Powerpro (12-pound mono diameter). This rod is handy for throwing larger live bait and lures. Although it seems a bit light, it is quite capable of handling larger fish and has landed fish up to 40 inches.

Casting

Legend Inshore #LIC70LM
This 7-foot rod is used for presentation of smaller lures and weedless plastics between ⅛ and ⅜ ounces. It is rated for line test from 6 to 12 pounds. This rod is combined with a Citica 100 DSV reel spooled with 20-pound test Powerpro (6-pound mono diameter). It casts the same lures as the comparable spinning model prior (⅛ to ⅜ ounces). This rod is great for weedless plastics in freshwater.

Legend Inshore #LIC70MLF
This 7-foot rod is rated for 8- to14-pound test lines. It is used for presentation of smaller jigs and lures between ⅛ and ½ ounces. For this rod, I use a Citica 200DPV spooled with 20-pound test Powerpro (6-pound mono diameter). This rod is almost always rigged with a ¼-ounce jig head. This allows me to change the tail as conditions change. In freshwater, this makes a nice rod for topwater buzzing soft plastics and frogs like Spro's Rojas Bronze Eye.

Legend Inshore #LIC70MF
This 7-foot rod is used for presentation of lures from ⅜ to ¾ ounces. This rod is rated for 8 to 17-pound lines. It is matched with a Curado 200DHSV reel spooled with 20-pound test Powerpro (6-pound mono diameter) I use this rod for topwater plugs, jigheads, and crank baits. I usually keep two rods of this size on my kayak—one with topwater, the other with a suspending lure, such as a mirrorlure or a corky. In freshwater, this is a great combination for fishing stinger worms, tubes, and buzzbaits.

Legend Inshore #LIC70MHF
This 7-foot rod is rated for lures from ½ to 1¼ ounces and 10 to 20-pound test lines. I matched this rod with the powerful Curado 300DSV reel spooled with 50-pound test Powerpro (12-pound mono diameter). It is used to throw larger topwaters, and on occasion weighted live bait rigs like a Carolina rig. Although not the heaviest rod I own, this rod has more than enough power and backbone to handle any fish that I may encounter on my adventures. In freshwater, this rod is used for bigger spinner baits, lures, and fishing heavy cover.

Fishing Lines

There are lots of fishing line types out there and the choices can vary with the individual angler's preference. The key is to balance the line to the specifications of the rod and reel. Most reels have at least three line sizes listed on the spool or box. I usually choose the middle line size. I personally prefer to use braided line with a fluorocarbon leader. Braided lines are much thinner than their monofilament counterparts, so you get the advantages of smaller diameter lines. For example, 8-pound Powerpro has the diameter of 1-pound test mono. I recommend buying braided lines for your kayak fishing reel according to the diameter not the pound test. This way you have a higher weight capacity, but the same line diameter as recommended by the reel manufacturer. Before you spool the braid onto the reel, use a length of light mono to act as a breakaway, and to prevent the braid from spinning on the spool. I use an Albright knot to attach the braid at the breakaway and the leader and use leader material that is matched to the terminal tackle. I typically carry 8, 10, 20, and 30-pound fluorocarbon leader material. The good thing about fluorocarbon is that even the heavier test lines almost disappear underwater. Caution: lighter test braid can cut you. Try to avoid wrapping the line around your finger or grabbing the braid while landing a fish.

Terminal Tackle

The choices for terminal tackle are endless, and too much for me to go over in this book. However, there are a few basic rigging techniques that work for me. It is very important to make sure your knots are dressed and hold fast. Sloppy knots lead to lost fish. There are several knots out there for attaching terminal tackle, choose the best knot that works for you. I almost always use the loop knot. It is basically a bowline knot. I like it because the loop allows the lure to move more naturally. The exceptions are topwater poppers and walk the dog lures. For these I use the Trilene knot. It prevents the line from fowling on the lure's treble hooks as it is worked along the surface.

Being a tournament angler, I tend to carry too much tackle. My advice is to carry as much as you are safely capable of carrying, but less is better. A good organizational technique, especially if you fish the same area, is to eliminate any tackle that you did not use on the prior trip. Soon you will find that you can be productive with just a few lures.

On the occasion that I fish live bait, I use the Carolina rig. (See Knots and Rigs section.) Instead of tying the braid directly to the leader, I put an egg sinker on the braid, add a bead (to prevent the swivel from going through the sinker), then tie it to a swivel, and tie the leader to the swivel. I use a Palomar knot for both the braid and the leader. I usually snell a circle hook to the 2 to 6-foot leader. For bottom bouncing, I use a 3-way swivel with the weight on the bottom. (See the Drop-shot and Halibut rig in the Knots and Rigs section.) This rig is great for structure fishing for wreck fish such as tautog and sea bass.

Having the right fishing equipment can make or break a kayak fishing trip.

Bait Handling and Storage

I'll begin with ways to keep bait fresh. After all you got to have good bait to catch big fish. The majority of anglers are used to cut bait, such as squid and cut mullet. The best way to keep cut bait fresh is to keep it in a small container with a small ice pack. I use a combination bait box and cutting board by Plano and add a reusable ice pack. I precut all my bait so that all I need to do is to put it on the hook. In kayak fishing, the more you prepare before you get on the water, the more time you spend fishing versus rigging. I prefer a separate container for my bait and keep cooler space for lunch. There is nothing worse than sodas and sandwiches that taste like bait.

Live bait is a bit harder to keep alive. The best and most economical way to keep them happy is to use a float and troll type minnow bucket. I put it overboard while fishing and pull it onto my kayak while paddling. I have no trouble keeping hardier minnows, such and gudgeons and mullet, alive this way. When live bait fishing, I carry this bucket along with my cast net. On hot days I use the Fish-Flo$_2$™ aerator system. This system consists of a commercially available oxygen tank, regulator, hose, and an air stone. This setup keeps my bait lively no matter what the conditions. One small tank will last about 24 hours. The other option is to buy or build a live well system for your kayak. I use a 2.5-gallon bucket with a 12-volt aerator. You can buy commercial systems made especially for a kayak. These are more expensive, but most are insulated and well worth the extra money.

For live bait such as mud minnows and mullet, you cannot beat a floating minnow bucket. Be sure to put it into the water often to keep your bait alive.

A resealable container with a refreezable ice block makes a great place to keep cut bait fresh.

Mesh bags like this are one way to keep bait alive and frisky. This one has a float and a weight to keep it vertical in the water column.

The Fish-Flo$_2^{TM}$ system can turn any bait bucket into an effective live well.

Hobie makes a self-contained live well system that uses the kayak's scupper hole to circulate water.

Food and Drinks

I find food and drink almost as important as tackle. Before I was called "ruthless" I was known as "snacks." I was always eating or planning on eating. That kind of metabolism is now gone, but I still keep some snacks tucked away for all-day trips.

The most important thing is hydration. Even if you don't bring food you should always bring water. I always carry two Nalgene bottles filled with water. Another option is to freeze commercially available water bottles. If packing a meal, I take two or three 24-ounce water bottles, pour out about 2-ounces, and freeze them solid. I use these to keep other items in my cooler cold and drink the water as it melts. This is a great way to carry water and not have the extra weight of melted ice or ice packs on the return trip.

Food is another individual choice. Many kayakers go for kayak-friendly prepackaged food, like Power Bars® and Snickers®. I prefer to save money and prepare my food at home. There is nothing like a PB&J or a nice BLT sandwich. For the latter, I use the two-compartment Tupperware containers, put the wet items (tomato slices and pickles) on one side and the dry items on the other. This container will keep your sandwich from getting soggy, from both the wet ingredients and from outside sources such as melted ice or condensation. Chips, cookies, and other snacks go in reusable Aloksak® bags. This way I have almost no waste to carry home. Everything goes in the dishwasher at the end of the day.

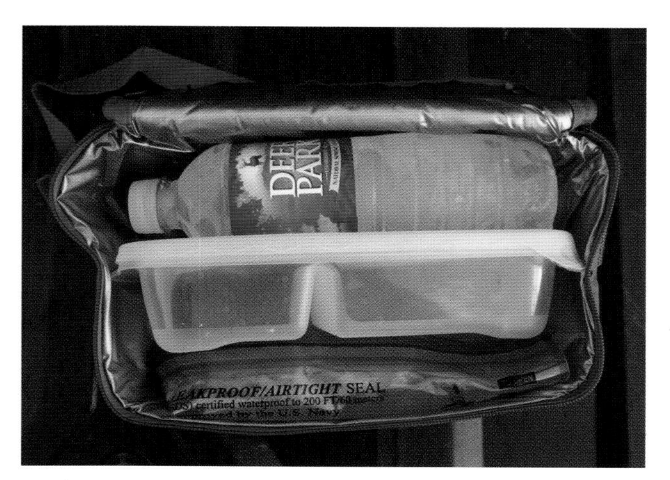

To keep your food cool use frozen water bottles. You can also drink the water as it melts.

Fishing in Unfamiliar Places

As a competition kayak angler, I have fished in some truly amazing areas. I have managed to catch fish and even place in tournaments with as little as one day of pre-fishing. How do I do it? Let's just say with a little bit of luck and a lot of planning. At first I had very little success. I would simply ask someone where the fish were biting and go to those areas. Well, let's just say that in competitions, lots of misinformation goes around. So eventually I started using the techniques that I use locally every day (after all, I do have a marine biology degree), and I started to catch fish. The more I planned and started to think like a fisheries biologist, the more successful I became. So here are a few pointers that can make fishing a new area successful, or at the least, educational.

Lay of the Land

Having maps and charts of the area that you are going to fish is a must. It will allow you to scope out areas that can hold fish as well as indicate access points, structure, markers, and any hazards. Some charts even give water depth and bottom composition. With the advent of the Internet, there is now a wealth of information out there. I purchased a commercial software program that gives me detailed charts of local areas. I have both topographic and marine charts with this program. If you want to go the free route, there are downloadable charts and software available from several sources on the Internet.

Nothing beats a good chart and Google Earth for scouting out potential honey holes.

Aerial and satellite photography is also available online. My favorite site is Google Earth. This site will allow you to zoom in very close, so close in fact, that you can tell what type of car is sitting at the boat ramp. I like it because you can see areas of shallow water, submerged vegetation, channels, and submerged structure. It is easy to pick out the fishy places with these resources. The basic service is free but has limited capabilities and the subscription service is definitely worth the extra money. You can also copy many of the maps, which is handy if you do not want to ruin a chart. Use weatherproof paper and you have a handy set of portable maps that might just get you out of a pinch.

Intelligence Gathering

Once you have studied your maps it is time to do some research. One of the best ways is to hire a guide, but this can be expensive, so the next best thing is to talk to someone local. Most anglers are willing to give up some limited information, which may be enough if you studied your maps. I prefer to Google "fishing (your destination)." I also look for message boards for the specific areas. There I will ask questions or even "lurk" to get info on all the hot spots. Anglers are prone to brag, so take advantage of it. Don't forget to ask about tackle used and the water conditions.

Conditions

There are several factors that affect fishing. Probably the most important are the environmental conditions: Tide, current, weather, solunar phase, and water quality.

Tide and current are very important factors. There are several places to get this information specific to your area. We fish some pretty skinny water, so getting caught in a low-tide situation can lead to a long walk home. I prefer to fish the incoming, slack high, and outgoing tides. I try to launch in an area that will allow me to ride the tide in, fish high tide, and then ride the outgoing back to the launch. This technique has never left me high and dry. I also prefer to fish when and where there is moving water. I never overlook cuts and culverts where there may be a little current. Not knowing the speed and direction of a current can also make a short paddle very long. Unfortunately during tournaments there is a time limit, so you are stuck with a window that may not allow for ideal tide and current conditions. Knowing exactly what they are will allow you to determine optimum fishing for that window.

Weather is a no-brainer, I actually wear a watch that shows barometric pressure and trends. I know that if it shows a major change in pressure, weather change is imminent. I also check the local marine weather forecast. Winds—heavy or light—can affect fishing conditions. For example, a light wind can blow the water off of a flat, which with a low tide can mean dragging a kayak for miles. It can also produce current, which may create an area that holds fish. Wind when combined with current can also make or break a kayak fishing trip. Wind and current going in the same direction may help you get to your spot or make it difficult to hold a position. Wind and current in opposite directions may hold you in one spot or create a dangerous chop. There are several more scenarios, but let's just say that knowing exactly what wind and current will be doing can make it easier to plan a trip.

Solunar phase tables are also a good reference. They use the phases of the sun and moon to determine the peak feeding times for fish. These are available online and in some GPS units. This method is not totally proven, but works with the tide to help determine a good time to fish.

Water quality information can be important in selecting areas to fish and tackle to use. Some relevant questions would be: Does the area have muddy or clear water? Was a recent fish kill due to red tide or pfisteria?

Target Fish

By understanding the fish you are chasing, you can even start to think like a fish. Before I go to an area, I prefer to read fishing guides and how-to books specific to the region. Magazines can also be a good source of information. Again the Internet contains a wealth of information. I especially like using results from marine research. There are numerous studies on feeding habits and preferred habitats for specific species. You can contact the local fisheries management agency to get the results of recent research.

Try to gain an edge by fully understanding the fish you are pursuing. Fly fishermen use the term "match the hatch." If you know what the fish are eating then you can match bait to that food source. I like to look in the water to see what species of bait are around. Whether it is fish or crustaceans, the most abundant bait will be obvious. At the end of the day, I also like to hang around fish cleaning stations and look at the contents of the stomach of certain species of fish. This is also a good place to glean information from proud anglers. Another option is to feel the belly of any fish that you plan to release. If you feel hard objects, they are eating crabs or shrimp; soft objects mean they are eating fish or other soft bodied invertebrates.

Know Yourself

Kayak fishing is a sport and, like all sports, you should know your limitations. As with all exercise, you should consult your doctor before starting. Knowing exactly how far and how fast you can paddle should always come into play. You would not want to paddle into a situation that you could not physically overcome, such as fighting a five-knot offshore current. Also do not take on large or dangerous fish without practice or at least an experienced buddy. I highly suggest a basic paddling course and a rescue course. These will make you more confident, which will get you on the water more and further develop your skills. Paddle even if the fishing is bad. Simply getting out and exploring will benefit you physically and mentally. You seem to notice more if you don't have a rod in your hand. Who knows, you might even find a new honey hole. One final point: always go with your gut instinct. If you are confident that an area or lure will produce, it will.

Fighting and Landing Fish

Kayak fishermen can enjoy larger fish just like fishermen in motorboats. Ocean Kayak team angler "Kayak Kevin" Whitley fights a trophy striped bass at the concrete ships at Kiptopeke State Park in Virginia.

The Hook Set

Probably the hardest part of catching a fish is getting the hook set. Using lures is a no-brainer, you usually know if the fish is hooked. The key is to keep tension on the line so that you will feel the strike. Slack lines can lead to missed hook-ups or swallowed lures. I smash or remove all barbs. It is better for the fish and for my clients. Barbs result in ended fishing trips and emergency room visits. Bait fishing is a bit different, but again proper line tension is the key. If you feel the strike you can get a solid hook-up and prevent a gut hook. I highly recommend circle hooks if you prefer to bait fish.

Fighting Fish

Once you are hooked up the best way to land the fish is to keep constant pressure on it and constantly change its direction by changing your rod angle. It is the change in direction that fatigues the fish and allows for a quick fight. Professional bass anglers commonly use this technique. I try to keep the fight to the front and sides of the kayak because I carry extra rods behind me and want to keep the fish away from these rods. You can use the fish to turn the kayak, which is especially true with bigger fish. The ideal position is from the side of the kayak. This is the area where most resistance is created. Fighting a fish from the front will lead to a "sleigh ride" and, unless you want to travel, is not the ideal way to fight a fish. In some instances the fish may change direction and go under the kayak. To counter the maneuver, put the rod tip out over the front of the kayak and clear the bow. Keep enough tension on the line to prevent a premature release. This is where the longer rods come into play. Once the line is cleared, continue to fish on the other side of the kayak. I have had many fish switch sides on me, so this technique is a good one to learn. Try not to land a fish that is too "green"—you might get a turtle instead of a fish. It is usually obvious when a fish is done, but always be prepared for one last run. When the fish is ready you'll be able to guide it to the side of your kayak for landing.

Catch and Release

The most common question I get is "what do you do with your fish?" As many know, I am a strong advocate of Catch, Photo, and Release (CPR). If you intend to release fish, the first step is to adjust your tackle for a quick fight. The quicker you land the fish the less stress you put on them. Use the stronger braided lines, such as Powerpro, to do this and use a heavier leader. I like to grab the monofilament leader in order to land the fish, as grabbing thin braided line could cut your hand. For light tackle rigs use 30-pound Powerpro and a leader made of 15- or 20-pound fluorocarbon. I adjust my drag to guarantee a quick fight and prefer to smash barbs on all terminal tackle. This serves a dual purpose. It allows for a quick release of fish and for you, if you happen to get hooked.

Once the fish is ready to be landed, a net offers more control over the fish once it's in the net. You are less likely to lose the fish and tackle if the fish decides to dance. I simply use my rod to guide the fish to the mouth of the net. Once in the net, I place the rod in a rod holder and prepare to land the fish. Try to leave the fish in the water while removing the hook. I occasionally use my lip gripper in conjunction with the net to assure that the fish does not get away, which is important in CPR tournaments. There are several methods to

Even smaller fish can give a great fight in a kayak. Angler David Hottel fights a nice skinny water redfish.

remove a hook, I prefer to use needle-nose pliers, like Shimano Baysteel pliers. I also keep an X-tools dehooker on board for deeper hooked fish. After the hook is removed use the net to cradle the fish and lift it onto the kayak for a photograph. Once under control on the kayak, use the lip gripper and support the fish's midsection with my free hand. I lay it on the ruler and photograph. You can use the above steps with just the lip gripper, but you stand the

Most fish will lie perfectly still when cradled in your hand like this.

The author prepares to release a nice redfish. Notice how he cradles the fish by its midsection. Photo by Mark Lozier.

The author demonstrates the best way to photograph a fish you plan to catch and release. Photo by Francois Betoulaud.

If a fish seems exhausted, hold it by the tail and pump it back and forth until it revives.

Using a lip gripper is a good way to hold a fish in the water until it revives.

chance of losing the fish. This method is good for any hero photos to show your buddies. After a quick photo or two use the two-hand cradle to return the fish to the water. In the water release the lip gripper, but continue to hold the fish by its midsection. If everything goes quickly, the fish will rapidly swim away. If it doesn't, slide your hand down to the tail and pump the fish back and forth in the water. After a few minutes the fish will swim away.

The rules change for larger fish. Use a folding net as a gauge. It should hold up to a 30-inch fish. If the fish is too big for the net use the leader to control the fish and then use the lip gripper. Always use caution, as the fight may not be over when you think it is. A locking rod holder, such as a Scotty, is a good place to put the rod while landing the fish. I try to get the fish to swim alongside of my kayak and use the lip gripper. One option is to use a gaff. This is okay as long as you properly lip gaff the fish. For catch and release, I find the lip gripper to be just as effective and a lot safer than the gaff. Lifting big fish can lead to a capsizing situation and no one wants that. Use your leg as support and pull the big fish (horizontally) onto your lap.

The key to landing big fish is to keep the fish low. Kevin Whitley used this "leg scoop" to land a trophy striped bass.

Angler/philosopher Jimbo Meador of Legacy Paddlesports with a boundary lakes pickerel. Photo by Mark Anders.

TKAA co-founder Darrell Hollifield with a nice mess of Yellow perch.

Wilderness Systems Team angler Chad Hoover wrestling a monster largemouth bass. Keep an eye out for his upcoming book on bass fishing from kayaks. Photo courtesy of Chad Hoover.

Saltwater Fishing

Saltwater fish tend to be larger and fight harder than freshwater fish. Using the proper techniques and gear can assure a catch of a lifetime. Here "Kayak Kevin" Whitley displays a great striped bass.

I have been a fan of saltwater fishing from early on. In my youth, we lived about six hours from my grandparents' vacation trailer in Topsail Beach, North Carolina. We would make that drive on a Friday night and come home on Sunday. Needless to say, we maximized our time by playing and fishing in the ocean and surrounding marshes. I have lots of fond memories about that area. I hated leaving and remember vowing that when I grew up I would live near the beach. Well at 35 I haven't quite yet grown up, but I do live and work near the salt.

In the last 10 years I have worked on and around saltwater, both professionally and for fun. My professional career has included fisheries research and data collection, recreational license fund administration, and most recently water quality monitoring. Combine that with a few days per week fishing, I consider myself a pretty experienced waterman. There are a few things to be aware of while kayak fishing in saltwater. Keep your eye on these and I guarantee a great and successful fishing trip.

Tides and Currents

Tides are the periodic rise and fall of sea levels. Tides are basically the respiration of the marine environment. The tides bring in fresh seawater that helps flush and dilute pollutants in estuaries. This water also helps the ecosystem by mixing well-oxygenated and nutrient rich seawater into estuarine environments. Tides bring in food for organisms from algae to striped bass. Areas with lots of tidal influence tend to have better water quality and better fishing.

All saltwater anglers, but especially the kayak angler, must appreciate tides. In order to assure a successful and safe trip, you must consider the effect the tide will have on the fish, as well as the paddle. As far as fishing success, most feeding cycles depend on the tide cycle. The tidal movement of water often is a deciding factor in where fish will feed, especially inshore environments most often fished by kayak anglers. As far as the paddle, it is good to know if you are going to have the tides working for or against you.

Typically anglers classify the tide in 4 stages:

- *High.* The tide is at its highest point.
- *Ebb.* The tide is going out.
- *Low.* The tide is at its lowest point.
- *Flood.* The tide is coming in.

In the periods of high and low water when there is no water movement, we call that *slack tide*. Other factors also affect tide, such as the structure of the ocean bottom and the geography of the continents. These factors are pretty static and most predictions take this into consideration. The weather can also affect the tide. Storm surges and wind can delay or advance the times of tidal activity and amplify the effects. As an example, in Lynnhaven Inlet, a south wind would cause tides to lower rapidly and stay low throughout the cycle. A north wind would cause a quicker rise in tide and higher than normal high tides. Knowing the current is no less important than knowing the tides. Like the tides, currents are affected by the moon and their speed can be related to lunar cycles. There are two different types of tidal currents. *Spring tides* are at their maximum current a few days after a new or full moon. *Neap tides* are at their weakest a few days after the quarter moons. Current affects both the fish and the paddle. I prefer to fish when the currents are moderate. I like enough water movement to stimulate feeding, but not too much that paddling is a burden. I want to be able to get home without having rubber arms.

A lot of folks ask me which tide is my favorite. There is no definite answer. Different locations and conditions will change my favorite tide cycles. As a rule I like to fish through a tide change. For example, when fishing in estuaries, I like to launch near the inlet, drift fish in on the flood, fish the flats at high tide and the beginning of the ebb, fish most of the ebb, and drift back to my launch area. This is a great time to maximize fishing and minimize paddling against the currents. This is the pattern I follow on my charters. As a rule, fish like to conserve energy and choose not to fight heavy current, so do I.

Tide and current patterns vary all over the world. The important thing is to find a fairly accurate resource for tidal predictions. My first choice is the NOAA site at http://tidesandcurrents.noaa.gov/.

Surf Launches and Landings

Probably one of the sure-fire ways to earn your turtle sticker is by doing a surf launch. The areas just beyond the breakers can offer an excellent opportunity for the kayak angler, but this can come at a heavy price. The surf zone is so unpredictable that most hard-core kayak anglers store their gear inside their kayak until they get outside the breakers.

George Hughes surfing in his SINK.

stepping on buried rays. This way you do not pin the ray down and cause it to sting. If you are hit, the best treatment is to put the injury under very hot water and seek medical attention. You may need a tetanus shot.

Oysters and Barnacles

In my 10+ years of kayak fishing, the most common injuries are caused by oysters, barnacles, and other sharp or pointy objects. I have seen several cases of massive lacerations caused by these seemingly harmless things. The problem is folks not wearing proper footwear. All kayak anglers should wear some sort of protective footwear, especially if you are going to wade areas with unknown bottom composition. A pair of sandals is not ideal footwear, but better than nothing. I prefer to wear wading shoes or booties. Not only are they designed to protect you from cuts and punctures, but help prevent sunburn on the tops of your feet. The problem with cuts and punctures in saltwater is that just about every inch of submerged material is covered with bacteria. Any injury should be cleaned with an antiseptic and treated with antibiotic ointment. If you have problems, see a doctor and indicate what caused the infection. There are antibiotics that are especially good for treating marine-related infections.

Having the proper footwear can protect both the top and the bottoms of your feet. NRS makes a variety of specialized footwear.

Finding Fish in Saltwater

Just like in freshwater, most saltwater fish tend to be structure oriented. In the salt, structure can be a number of things, natural or manmade. On the flats, structure can be grass islands, submerged aquatic vegetation (SAV), oyster beds, shell piles, crab pots, piers, and docks. All of these types of structure will hold fish. When I fish unknown shallow water locations this is what I look for, especially SAV. The next things to look for are cuts and channels that drain from large flats. These places tend to funnel bait to a small area and are usually ambush points for predatory fish. Deep channels that run next to flats are also ambush points. Predatory fish will often stay near these channels for security. I often sight cast to fish cruising the flats near these channels.

Sometimes you can use other animals to find fish. "Nervous water" is when baitfish anticipate an attack and begin to ball up near the surface. This is a good sign that bigger fish are near by. Nervous water often leads to a blitz, which is when predatory fish crash the surface while feeding. Birds will often lead you to a blitz. Seeing birds massing over the water is a good sign that predatory fish are blitzing. With birds, the thing to remember is that some species (like Gannets) can dive to great depths to catch baitfish and don't necessarily indicate that predatory fish are there. Look for a mixture of bird species together, which is a good sign. If you are fortunate

Another sign of feeding fish is feeding birds. Seeing boils and birds working bait like this is sure-fire sign that big predatory fish are feeding.

One of the most sought out signs of feeding fish, tailing is a great indicator of feeding redfish.

you can paddle to them before they disperse. Do not paddle through blitzing fish, stay on the outside and cast into the frenzy.

Another way that fish give themselves up is by tailing or mudding. Tailing is where fish root around the bottom for crustaceans. They are waving their tails to you and saying, "here I am," and "I am eating." Also look for plumes of mud in clear water, a good sign that fish are feeding.

In open water, structure still holds fish, but may not be close. In this case, we often use chum. Chum is nothing more than ground up fish or other things in a mesh bag. It is placed in the water to attract fish. Attach chum to a separate anchor and float in open water. I do not attach it to my kayak. There are big critters out there and I don't want an unintentional sleigh ride. In shallow water, I place my chum on a flat away from the kayak and cast in that area.

One of my favorite ways to find fish is at night. Here in Virginia Beach there are several bridges and waterfront properties that are lit up like Christmas trees. Baitfish and crustaceans are attracted to these lights and so are the predatory fish. Quite often the light creates a "light line" in the water. Fish can be found stacked up like cord wood in these shadows. A good example is the Hampton Roads Bridge Tunnel (HRBT). You can literally paddle up to and grab these fish by the tail. It is not uncommon for an angler to catch a striped bass on every cast.

The best way to find fish is to get intel before leaving home. The Internet has lots of resources. I like to call on the local tackle shops and see what's biting and which bait is working. I also like to scout out the public boat ramps and fish cleaning stations. Fishermen cleaning a mess of fish are usually in a good mood and most are ready to brag about their day's catch. Pay close attention to the stomach contents.

Fishing with Bait

Most saltwater anglers choose to fish with live or dead bait. This is a sure fire way to catch fish, but sometimes you have to sort through smaller fish and other nuisances. It is not my preferred way to fish, but sometimes comes through in a pinch. There are many ways to fish bait but the most common is with a Carolina rig or a double hooked bottom rig. Bait fishing is very effective, but is more detrimental to fish that are released. This is caused by fish getting gut hooked from swallowing the bait. The best way to avoid this is to use circle hooks. Circle hooks are designed to allow the fish to hook itself, without any help from the angler. Properly rigged and fished circle hooks almost always hook the fish in the lips. I very rarely use bait, but when I do I always use circle hooks and always have the rod in my hands not in a rod holder.

Fishing with Lures

I am an avid light tackle angler and own more lures than anyone could throw in a weekend. Just about every saltwater fish will take a lure if presented properly. Just like in freshwater, the best tactic is to "match the hatch." If you can actively see fish feeding and if you have something similar to size and shape to the prey, chances are the fish will eat it. Also if you see baitfish swimming around you, it might be a good idea to match these as well. Not every situation will give you an opportunity to see the bait. In this case you have to go with what I call a fish finder lure. A fish finder lure is a lure that in some way attracts fish. My favorite fish finder lures are lures that move lots of water and/or make lots of vibration. A good example is a topwater lure, such as a Rapala Skitterwalk, or a spinner bait type lure. I use a riptide mullet on a hand-made gold #3 Colorado blade. These lures create a commotion that most fish cannot resist. For deeper water, I use a RipTide® mullet or a Rapala® X-rap. Another way to create a fish finder lure is to add scent to lures you commonly use. I'll coat both hard and soft baits with Smelly Jelly® or spray them with RipTide® Blast. Other alternatives are to use soft baits like Fishbites®, Berkley® Gulps, and FoodSource. These baits are made of natural materials and scents that fish cannot ignore. These baits are effective but tend to attract "pickers" and tend to get chewed up or bitten off.

Saltwater Tackle

The types of rods can vary according to the type of fishing you do. For open water bait fishing I use the heavy spinning or casting outfits in the 20- to 30-pound class. The majority of my fishing is on the flats. For this I carry at least three rods, one light spinner for weedless soft baits and two spinning rods—one with a topwater lure and the other with a subsurface lure. I prefer to change rods rather than change lures. Tying on lures just takes too much time and may cause me to miss an opportunity. During tournaments I carry five rods. I know it seems excessive, but trust me it is effective.

Saltwater Lures

Jerk Baits

These are very effective in shallow areas where there is a need for a weedless finesse presentation. An erratic retrieve with lots of long pauses will yield good results. These baits are designed with a special hook pocket that allows the bait to be fished in areas with lot of cover. It is a great lure for casting in and around docks at night. I like the darker colors. This bait can also be rigged with a jighead or a weighted weedless hook for a deeper presentation. This is a great way to fish for bottom dwellers like flounder.

Shrimp and Crab Lures

These lures imitate crabs and shrimp. They can also be rigged weedless or with a jighead. The key is to fish the bait slowly, so it looks like a swimming shrimp. A popular inshore method is to use a popping cork with the shrimp patterns.

Paddle Tail Minnows

This is my go to lure. I always keep a rod rigged with a paddle tail on a jighead. Sizes generally go from 3 to 5 inches and come in a variety of colors. I try to carry four different colors that include chartreuse, white, natural, and a wild color like pumpkinseed with chartreuse tail or electric chicken. Use the right weight jighead for the depth you are fishing (lighter for shallow, heavier for deeper). I vary retrieves until I get a strike.

Curly Tail Grubs

In addition to paddle tails, I always carry a curly tailed grub. These lures are fished just like paddle tails, but have more action and slower speeds. These are also great lures for drifting in the current.

Saltwater Spinner and ChatterBait™

Once freshwater standards, spinner and chatter baits are becoming effective lures in the saltwater arsenal. For spinnerbaits, I build my own arms and add different types of blades. I simply attach these to the paddle tails and grubs mentioned above. I call this my Cajun fish finder. Chatter baits are also effective, but tend to foul up more than the spinner baits. I use chatter baits in deeper open waters.

Spoons

An old standard, all shallow water kayak anglers should have a few good spoons in their boxes. Nemire even makes spoons with rattles and spinners. A popular method is to rig the spoons with a trailer, which are deadly on most shallow-water fish.

Topwater Lures

Another shallow water standard, these include topwater walking and popping lures. I prefer the walking type lure like the Skitterwalk and the spook lures. They seem more like a baitfish to me and don't spook fish like poppers.

Subsurface Lures

These lures work lower in the water column and are effective in shallow and deeper waters. Good examples are the MirrOlure® minnows and corkys. They typically suspend in the water column and can be counted down to reach deeper depths. I like slow retrieves with pauses and an occasional jerk—think wounded fish!

Deep Lures

These are either lipped or weighted lures. The lips are often large and carry the lures to certain depths according to the retrieve speed. Most of these lures are used when trolling. Good examples are the X-rap and the Rat-L-Trap.

Tube and Worm

Kind of a crossover between trolling and bait fishing, this common method uses a piece of tubing with a treble hook at the end. The hook is usually baited with a sand worm for flavor. It is commonly used in the Northeast when trolling for striped bass, bluefish, and grey trout.

Saltwater soft plastics, spoons, and spinner baits.

Saltwater topwater lures.

Saltwater subsurface and deep diving lures.

Plastic kayak meets concrete ships in the lower Chesapeake Bay.

Favorite Fishing Locations

Photo by Chad Hoover.

Lighthouse Lakes

Aransas Pass, Texas

There is nothing like a Texas redfish, and Lighthouse Lakes is the place to catch them. Photo by Dean Thomas.

General Info

I fished my first big kayak fishing tournament in this area. This is were I met Dean "Slowride" Thomas who I consider to be one of the major driving forces in kayak fishing today. Dean has been guiding trips in and around Aransas Pass for several years. One of the most popular fishing areas in the vicinity is Lighthouse Lakes. These shallow flats have vast expanses of crystal clear water and grass beds. Lighthouse Lakes has a great series of marked paddling trails that by themselves will make for a great day on the water. Add to that some great fishing, and you are set.

Fish Species

Redfish, spotted trout, black drum, sheepshead, ladyfish, and flounder are the most popular species. Lighthouse Lakes is a popular spot for tailing redfish.

Time to Go

This is a year-round fishery, but the peak times are in June to July and October to November.

Top Lures

- Topwater walking plugs, spook jr and skitterwalk jr (bone is the color)
- Shrimp imitations like the Realistic shrimp or the DOA ¼-ounce shrimp (clear/gold flake)
- 3- and 4-inch paddle tail minnows (white, chartreuse, and Pumpkin seed/chartreuse)

Top Flies

- Spoon flies like the Slowride Especial, size # 4-1/0
- Small poppers, size #6 (red, orange, chartreuse, and black)
- Clousers, size 2-2/0 (chartreuse/white, tan/white)
- Crab fly (size 4-1/0) (tan, olive)

Top Guides

Dean Thomas of Slowride Guide Services.

Tips

Wear waders or tuck your pants into your wading boots to avoid swimmer's itch, aka hydroids. Watch the tides, low water can make kayaking tough.

Difficulty

Texas has very good access, so getting to the launch site is pretty easy. Most of the boating traffic is around the Aransas and Lydia Ann Channels. Get into the lakes and motorboat traffic will be at a minimum. This area rates a difficulty of 2 on a scale of 1–10.

The author releases a nice skinny water redfish. Photo by Dean Thomas.

Ladyfish are considered a nuisance, but offer up a spectacular fight with lots of tail walking. Photo by Chad Hoover.

Getting to Lighthouse Lakes

From Rockport take Hwy 35 to Aransas Pass about 11 miles. Turn left on Texas Hwy 361. Continue on Hwy 361 over the bridge and out the causeway to the Lighthouse Lakes Paddling Trails Park on the left. For more info check out http://www.tpwd.state.tx.us/fishboat/boat/paddlingtrails/coastal/lighthouse_lakes/#getthere

- Phone: 361-758-3111
- GPS: 27°51'55.56" N, 97°04'58.54" W

Cockroach Bay

Tampa, Florida

General Info

I was introduced to Cockroach Bay while at a kayak fishing tournament in 2004. I fell in love with the area and have returned to fish there in other tournaments. Called "Cockroach Bay" because of the abundance of horseshoe crabs, it is owned and operated by the Hillsboro Port Authority. This preserve has two marked paddling trails and offers some of the best scenic kayak fishing in Florida. Cockroach Bay covers more than 8,000 acres and has numerous mangrove islands that provide habitat for several gamefish species. Submerged habitats include seagrass beds, hardbottom, and oyster reefs. Cockroach Bay is not a motor-restricted area but most of this preserve is too shallow for motorboats.

Fish Species

Redfish, spotted trout, and snook are the most sought after species. Occasionally you will find cobia, jacks, ladyfish, flounder, Spanish mackerel, and tarpon.

Time to Go

Cockroach Bay has great fishing year-round, but the warmer months have more aggressive, hungry fish.

Top Lures

- Topwater walk the dog lures
- Shallow swimming crankbaits
- Gold spoons

The author with his first snook. This fish spun his kayak twice and jumped completely over the bow. Photo by Dave Moss.

Dave Moss with a scrappy Cockroach Bay snook.

- Jerk shads on weighted and unweighted weedless hooks
- Shrimp imitations on ⅛-oz hooks
- 4-inch paddle tail minnows (chartreuse, white, natural, and pumpkin seed with chartreuse tail)

Top Flies

- Clousers, size 1/0 and 2/0 (chartreuse/white) and (olive/white)
- Crab patterns, size 1/0 (olive and tan)
- Poppers, size 1/0 (all white or all black)

Top Guides

Steve Gibson of Southern Drawl Charters. See guide section for more information.

Tips

Fish near mangroves for redfish and snook. Go weedless or lose lots of lures. Early in the morning fish around the many cuts that open out into Tampa Bay as large trout can be seen cruising these areas. Keep an eye out for manatees (an endangered marine mammal)!

Difficulty

The launch area has a high occurrence of break-ins. Most occur at night. Local authorities regularly patrol the area. Keep your vehicle locked and your valuables out of sight. The weekend brings lots of traffic, so fish during the week if possible. Boating traffic can be heavy in the main channels. Given the crowded nature of the ramp, the area is worth the minor inconveniences you may encounter. I give Cockroach Bay a 3 on my difficulty scale of 1–10.

Getting to Cockroach Bay

From Tampa Bay take 41 south (South Tamiami Trail) through Ruskin. Turn right (West) at Cockroach Bay Road and drive until you reach the end. Ramp is located at 5298 Cockroach Bay Road.

- Phone: 813-671-7754
- GPS: 27°41'13.45" N, 82°31'13.47" W

Jamaica Bay

New York City

General Info

Definitely the most urban of all my favorite locations, my first impressions of Jamaica Bay were not great. All that changed once I left the hustle and bustle of the city and paddled out onto this beautiful fishery. I was amazed by clear water and breaking fish in less than 4 feet of clear water. Just like Texas, but with northern Atlantic fish species. To the untrained eye, Jamaica Bay looks no different than any other coastal estuary. It has scattered grass islands with mud and sand-bottomed marshes. But look closely on the horizon and you can see the New York City skyline, complete with the Empire State Building.

Fish Species

Popular species include striped bass, false albacore, bluefish, tautog (blackfish), and grey trout.

Time to Go

The striped bass action starts in early May and into June. The water quality improves as spring progresses. In June the clear water allows sight fishing for big stripers and bluefish. In July and August warm water temps tend to slow down the action, however small bluefish can be found inside the bay. In late August the false albacore make a showing in the mouths of the bays. In September and October the larger striped bass and bluefish return to the marshes, the peak time is the last half of October. Fishing continues through November but slows as the fish begin their southerly migration. December can be good but is very weather dependent.

Top Lures

- 4- and 5-inch paddle tail minnows on ½- and ¾-oz jigheads (white, chartreuse, and natural colors)
- Jerk shads on unweighted worm hooks or on ½- and ¾-ounce jigheads (white, chartreuse, pink, and natural colors)
- Rat-L-Traps®
- Topwater popping and walk the dog lures (natural colors and chartreuse). Make sure to use a wire leader for toothy bluefish.

Kayaks and anglers ready for a day of fishing on Jamaica Bay in New York City.

Top Flies

- Sand eel and silverside patterns, size 2/0 (grey/white or olive /white, with flash down side)
- Deceivers or Half and Halfs, size 2/0-4/0 (white, chartreuse, natural)
- Clousers, size 1/0 and 3/0 (chartreuse/white, grey/white, olive/white)

Top Guides

John Fisher of River Bay Flyfishing.

Tips

Look for birds feeding, definitely a sign of feeding striped bass and bluefish. Grey trout tend to feed a bit deeper. Try bottom bouncing a pink bucktail or jerk shad of ⅜ to 1 ounce. The channels between the many islands also hold fish. Keep an eye out for undercut banks.

Difficulty

Jamaica Bay is a vast expanse of shallow water, so winds can whip up some nasty swells. Currents are moderate but not hard to negotiate. Be prepared for longer paddles if you want to find the areas that get less pressure. On calm days Jam Bay can be a paddler's paradise, definitely the jewel of New York City. I give Jamaica Bay a difficulty of 4 on a scale of 1–10.

Getting to Jamaica Bay

The worst part about getting to Jamaica Bay is the traffic and the tolls. They go up if you are pulling a trailer. However the great fishing will more than make up for that expense.

Floyd Bennet Field is a great place to access Jamaica Bay. It is located just off of Flatbush Avenue. It is the site of the Annual Jamaica Bay Kayak Fishing Tournament. From the Belt Parkway in Brooklyn take exit 11-S which brings you onto Flatbush Avenue South. Keep left and turn left at the traffic light just before the Marine Parkway Bridge toll plaza.

- Phone: 718-338-3799
- GPS: 40°35'45.39" N, 73°52'51.70" W

Eric Evans fights a feisty bluefish in New York.

Lynnhaven Inlet

Virginia Beach, Virginia

Lynnhaven Inlet from the air. This photo was taken on approach to Norfolk International Airport.

General Info

The Lynnhaven River system is a tidal estuary. Connecting to the Chesapeake Bay just west of Cape Henry at Lynnhaven Inlet, it is a moderately developed watershed that spans about 64 square miles. At one time it was world renowned for its oysters, which until late 2007 were condemned to harvest due to high fecal levels. Recent water quality in Lynnhaven has improved enough to allow shellfish harvest in designated areas. The Lynnhaven River system consists of three sections: the Eastern Branch, the Western Branch, and Broad Bay. Just about every fish common to coastal Virginia can be caught in Lynnhaven. With three public access sites, the area in general is very kayak friendly.

Fish Species

Red drum, black drum, croaker, spot, spotted trout, striped bass, flounder, sheepshead, tautog, and bluefish.

Time to Go

Lynnhaven is fishable year-round. Schoolie striped bass and bluefish will winter there if the temperatures stay mild. May usually brings all the listed species inside. In hotter months croaker, flounder, and redfish dominate the scene. From August through November, Lynnhaven has its best fishing. Many kayakers easily get multiple species slams (spotted trout, flounder, and redfish) during this time. When the waters cool in November, the striped bass dominate again.

Top Lures

- 3- and 4-inch paddle tail minnows (pumpkin seed/chartreuse, white, and black/silver)
- Redfish Magic Spinner Baits (pumpkin seed/chartreuse tail)
- Topwater lures (bone, chartreuse, and black/silver)
- Jerk shads (chartreuse, white, shad)

Top Flies

- Clousers, size 2/0 (chartreuse/white, tan/white, olive/orange, red/orange, and black)
- Rattling Shrimp, size 2/0 (white, chartreuse, and pink)
- Bendbacks, size 1/0 and 2/0 (chartreuse, olive, red/chartreuse, and black)

Tips

Try to maximize your fishing time by fishing two hours before and after the high tides. On the outgoing tide, set up outside small creeks that drain into the main channels. At night try fishing the lighted docks. Use black flies and lures and you won't be disappointed.

Difficulty

Lynnhaven has both dangerous and benign areas. The most dangerous is Lessner Bridge, where all the water from the Lynnhaven River system ebbs and floods to the Chesapeake Bay. The current can be fierce here and boat traffic heavy. The main channels can also have strong currents and heavy boat traffic. However, there are lots of shallow flats that see almost no boat traffic and plenty of winding creeks to navigate. Getting to these areas can be a challenge, though worth the effort. On a 1–10 scale, I would rate Lynnhaven a 5.

Getting to Lynnhaven Inlet

Lynnhaven Boat Ramp, also called the Crab Creek Ramp, is located at 3576 Piedmont Circle and is city owned. It will cost you $2.00 to park. This facility is closest to the inlet and only a short paddle from world class fishing.

- Phone: 757-460-7590
- GPS: 36°54'25.56" N, 76°05'44.77" W

First Landing State Park is located off 64th street in Virginia Beach. Go west from 64th and Atlantic Avenue on 343. This state-operated park offers great access to the Broad Bay section of the Lynnhaven River.

- Phone: 757-412-2300
- GPS: 36°53'24.94" N, 76°01'03.86" W

Hutton Circle Launch is an urban canoe and kayak launch area that offers access to the headwaters of the Eastern Branch of the Lynnhaven River. It is located at 300 Hutton Circle.

- Phone: 757-385-1100 (Virginia Beach Parks and Recreation)
- GPS: 36°50'29.86" N, 76°03'24.90" W

Tarus Vebeluna with a huge Lynnhaven Inlet flounder. He won the flounder division of the TKAA kayak fishing tournament in 2006.

Hickory Mound Unit Big Bend WMA

Taylor County, Florida

Sunrise at Hickory Mound Unit of Big Bend WMA, these flats were crawling with redfish and spotted trout.

General Info

Hickory Mound is a 14,427-acre area located in Taylor County. It is part of the Big Bend Wildlife Management Area. It is also a part of the Big Bend Seagrasses Aquatic Preserve. I had the opportunity to spend time here during the 2008 FCKA kayak fishing tournament. As we paddled out, I was apprehensive of the dark muddy water until we got into the open water of the Gulf. The water cleared and the fish were everywhere. There are several creeks that open into the gulf, and a variety of habitats from oyster bars to grass beds. It offers a great fishery that is a very short paddle from the launch sites.

Fish Species

Flounder, spotted trout, and redfish.

Time to Go

Spotted sea trout are abundant in March and April and later in October and November. Redfish are available year-round with the best fishing in the cooler months.

Top Lures

- 3 and 4-inch paddle tail minnows (pumpkin seed/chartreuse, white, and black/silver)
- Redfish Magic spinner baits (pumpkin seed/chartreuse tail)
- Topwater lures (pink, bone, chartreuse, and black/silver)
- Jerk shads (chartreuse, white, shad)
- Spoons (pink is very popular)

Top Flies

- Clousers, size 2/0 (chartreuse/white, tan/white, olive/orange, red/orange, and black)
- Rattling shrimp, size 2/0 (white, chartreuse, and pink)
- Bendbacks, size 1/0 and 2/0 (chartreuse, olive, red/chartreuse, and black)

Top Guides

Jeff Suber of www.fcka.net, jeffsuber@yahoo.com, 850-210-9296.

Tips

For redfish and flounder, fish the creek openings. For larger trout, paddle out to the deeper clear waters.

Difficulty

Access here is very easy, and the fishing can be phenomenal. Be mindful of the winding creeks. A GPS or at least a map is useful. Shallow waters limit the amount of motorboat traffic. Be sure to secure your valuables as these areas are used heavily. This location gets a difficulty of 2 on a scale of 1 to 10.

Getting to Hickory Mound

The Hickory Mound Unit of the Big Bend WMA is located off of Highway 98, about 20 miles west of Perry, Florida. Off of Hwy 98, look for Cow Creek Grade. This grade circles the Hickory Mound impoundment and offers two boat ramps for access. The second ramp gets less motorboat traffic.

- Phone: 386-758-0525
- GPS: 30°00'55.34" N, 83°52'04.85" W

Anglers spreading out to chase redfish and trout.

Hampton Roads Bridge Tunnel

Norfolk, Virginia

The Hampton Roads Bridge Tunnel, locally known as the HRBT, holds a variety of fish and is fishable year-round.

General Info

Truly an urban fishing experience, the Hampton Roads Bridge Tunnel (locally called the HRBT) can be one of the best fishing locations in the Tidewater Area of Virginia. Just minutes from Norfolk Naval Station (the world's largest naval base), the HRBT provides ample structure for most of the saltwater species common to Virginia's coastal waters. The HRBT consists of a bridge and tunnel complex that crosses the James River and creates a major artery from Norfolk to Hampton, Virginia. It has become one of the most popular kayak fishing destinations in Virginia.

Fish Species

Striped bass, grey trout, spotted trout, flounder, spot, croaker, bluefish, and red drum.

Time to Go

Smaller schoolie stripers (18–26 inches) hold year-round at the HRBT. They will feed every night during the peak current flow. Larger striped bass from 30 to 40 inches show up in February, March, and early April. During this time, shad and bluefish also offer hearty fights. Summertime brings flounder, croaker, grey trout and spotted trout. You can literally fill up your kayak with spot in the fall.

Top Lures

- 4 and 5-inch paddle tail minnows on ⅛- and ½-oz jigheads (white, chartreuse, and natural colors)
- Jerk shads on unweighted worm hooks or on ⅛- and ½-ounce jigheads (white, chartreuse, and natural colors)
- 4-inch curly tail minnows (white, chartreuse, and natural colors)
- Topwater popping and walk the dog lures (bone and black/silver)

Top Flies

- Clousers, size 1/0 and 2/0 (chartreuse/white, gray/white, olive/white, and black at night)
- Deceivers, size 2/0 (chartreuse/white, gray/white, olive/white, and black at night)

Top Guides

Cory "Ruthless" Routh of Ruthless Fishing Inc.

Tips

Go at night and take advantage of the feeding fish in the light line. Approach from the shadows so you do not spook the fish, and look for and cast to the larger fish. A true sight casting fishery, it is not hard to land a striper on every cast. Just like evening wear, the color for this nighttime fishery is black.

Difficulty

Depending on the lunar tide cycle and wind, the current at the HRBT can be strong. There are several shoals that cause tidal rips that can make kayak fishing hairy. Keep an eye on them and you should be fine. During striper season the boat traffic can be busy so keep an eye out for trolling motorboats. Most of the best fishing is at night. Make sure to lock up your vehicle.

Getting to HRBT

The HRBT is located on Highway 64 in Norfolk, Virginia. The best access is from the Willoby Spit boat ramp. The ramp is located on the 1200 block of Bayville Avenue in Norfolk, just east of the HRBT.

- GPS: 36°57'52.01" N, 76°17'16.59" W

Darrell Hollifield with a nice nighttime striper. Not even rain will stop these two from meeting.

Calvin Jordan with a nice stringer of spotted trout from the HRBT.

Lake Mattamuskeet

Hyde County, North Carolina

General Info

I had a great opportunity to get acquainted with Lake Mattamuskeet during my college years. East Carolina University has a field station there, so I got to help out with a few projects during my undergraduate studies. I also spent a summer there as an intern with the USFWS. It was during this time that I really had an opportunity to explore the lake. At 50,000 acres, Mattamuskeet is the largest natural lake in North Carolina. It spans about 15 miles from east to west and 7 miles from north to south, is fed by runoff, and is rumored to have its roots as an underground fire that burned for "18 moons." The lake is a major stop for migratory birds on the Atlantic Flyway. Lake Mattamuskeet also has a marked paddling trail. This 9-mile trail is part of the Albemarle Region Canoe and Small Boat Trails System. It is located on the south shore of Lake Mattamuskeet. Even if the fishing gets slow, the scenery and wildlife will more than make up for a bad day of fishing.

Fish Species

Popular species include largemouth bass, striped bass, catfish, bream, and other species. There are four canals that connect Lake Mattamuskeet to the Pamlico Sound. Saltwater species such as croaker, striped bass, and ladyfish can also be caught. Mattamuskeet also has some of the largest blue crabs that you will ever find. Herring dipping and blue crab fishing at the water control structures is a very popular pastime of the local community. Bow fishing for carp, bowfin, and gar is permitted during the fishing season as well.

Once a sporting icon in eastern North Carolina, the lodge at Lake Mattamuskeet still watches over this fishing paradise.

The culverts of the Mattamuskeet causeway are some of the best places to fish.

Time to Go

The lake is open to the public for boating from March 1 through November 1. Bank fishing and fishing Highway 94 culverts is allowed year-round. Fishing is good during most of this period. Local anglers prefer the spring and fall months, when the air and water temperatures are cooler. Fishing for bass, catfish, and bream is excellent in the canals and along the lakeshore in the spring and fall. Herring dipping is permitted from March 1 through May 15 and crab fishing is permitted year-round in certain areas.

Getting to Lake Mattamuskeet

Highway 264 is the main route traveling east to west. You can access Mattamuskeet from the north via Highways 45 and 94. Highway 94 becomes the causeway that bisects Lake Mattamuskeet and offers access and parking at each of the five culverts located along its path. There is a launch area just north of the Refuge entrance on Highway 94. The Mattamuskeet National Wildlife Refuge entrance, off Highway 94, is about one mile north of the intersection of Highways 264 and 94. Another launch area can be found behind the main office building.

- Phone: 252-926-4021
- GPS: 35°27'06.41" N, 76°10'33.52" W

Top Lures

- Spinner and buzz baits
- Jerk Shads
- Topwater popping and walk the dog lures
- Small Jigs

Top Flies

- Poppers
- Muddlers
- Hoppers
- Clousers

Top Guides

Cory “Ruthless” Routh of Ruthless Fishing Inc.

Tips

In the hotter months take some insect repellant. The lake has more green head flies than you can kill with a paddle. This is a great place to take a fly rod. A few poppers are all you will need. The canals surrounding the lakes are worth exploring so don’t hesitate to try fishing these areas.

Difficulty

Mattamuskeet is a kayak angler’s paradise. There is very little boating traffic and only a few areas with public access. The refuge offers parking and access via its launch area. There are plenty of fishing spots within a short paddle of this launch. I give Lake Mattamuskeet a difficulty of 3 on a scale of 1–10.

Eastern Shore of Virginia NWR

Cape Charles, Virginia

Chad Hoover putting the heat on something big.

General Info

Situated at the tip of the Delmarva Peninsula, the Eastern Shore of Virginia National Wildlife Refuge is the gateway to one of the best kayak fisheries in Virginia. Nestled between the Atlantic Ocean and Chesapeake Bay, this 1,123-acre refuge was established in 1984 for migratory and endangered species management and for wildlife dependent recreation including interpretation and education. It offers access to several types of saltwater fishing, from skinny water to the open ocean. Fisherman Island and Skidmore Island are closed to the public. Trespassing (including boat landing or walking on the beach) is prohibited on these two islands.

Fish Species

Flounder, spotted trout, grey trout, croaker, red drum, black drum, croaker, spot, sharks, and striped bass. During the summer, this is a nursery ground for big sharks, so be careful with bait or when landing fish.

Time to Go

Big striped bass are around from November through February. There is also a fishery for trophy red drum in the surf in early spring and late fall. Cut bait is the preferred way to fish for these behemoths. From late May through November, there is a variety of species available.

Top Lures

- Large gold spoons
- Rat-L-Trap® lures (menhaden and shad colors)
- 3- and 4-inch paddle tail minnows (pumpkin seed/chartreuse, white, and black/silver)
- Redfish Magic spinner baits (pumpkin seed/chartreuse tail)
- Topwater lures (bone, chartreuse, and black/silver)
- Jerk shads (chartreuse, white, shad)

Top Flies

- Clousers, size 2/0 (chartreuse/white, tan/white, olive/orange, red/orange, and black)
- Rattling Shrimp, size 2/0 (white, chartreuse, and pink)
- Bendbacks, size 1/0 and 2/0 (chartreuse, olive, red/chartreuse, and black
- Large Deceivers and Half and Halfs, Size 2/4-4/0 (white, chartreuse, and olive /white)

Top Guides

Cory Routh of Ruthless Fishing Inc.

Tips

Look for slicks on the water. These are caused by big redfish rooting around the bottom for food. Always fish this area with a buddy because it is a long way to help at this location. Don't overlook the mud banks, oyster beds and seagrass beds in this area. Watch the tides, as low water means quite a bit of mud slogging, especially on your return to the kayak launch.

Difficulty

This site offers several types of fishing. The inshore sites are relatively safe, but keep an eye on the winds. These shallow areas can build with the right wind direction and speed. There is decent fishing in the areas adjacent to the launch areas, but better fishing just a few miles from the launch. The inlets are very productive but the current can be strong, and the waves can get big and pose a danger if you choose to fish there. Stick inside the inlet and I'll give it a 5 (on a difficulty scale of 1–10), go out into the inlets and the surf zone and I'll give those areas an 8.

Getting to Eastern Shore of Virginia NWR

The refuge is located on Highway 13, just north of the Chesapeake Bay Bridge Tunnel toll booths. Enter the refuge and follow the main road past the visitor center. Follow the signs to the free kayak launch area. If that is full you can use the boat ramp for $10.00.

- Phone: 757-331-2760
- GPS:
  Kayak Launch 37°07'44.63" N, 75°57'17.35" W
  Boat Ramp 37°07'40.25" N, 75°56'59.75" W

Anglers set up to catch big eastern shore redfish. These fish can average 40–60 pounds.

Oahu, Hawaii

Issac Brumaghim with a nice Wahoo. Pelagic fish are just a short paddle away in Hawaii. Photo by Ed Kawasaki.

General Info

I visited Oahu in 2005, and although I did not fish from a kayak, I did get to do my share of fishing from the shore. I recognized the potential for a kayak here but did not have time to research the possibilities. Back in Virginia I set out do some research and found a few guides more than willing to help out. Most helpful was Isaac Brumaghim of Aquahunters. This group of anglers prefers to fish the West and North shores of Oahu. They typically target the pelagic species, but do well closer to shore also. They do very well catching mahi mahi, trevally, barracuda, and tuna species.

Oahu also has awesome fly fishing for giant bonefish on the flats of Kaneohe Bay. This is mostly a wade fishery, but the kayak makes for good transportation across these flats. Oahu also has a killer fresh water fishery in Lake Wilson, which is a great location for peacock bass, bream, and other species. It is a great place for the kayak. I am planning a return trip to Oahu in 2009. You can bet I'll be spending some of that time in a kayak at these locations.

Fish Species

Saltwater: trevally, bonefish, barracuda, ladyfish, milkfish, moi, mullet, mahi mahi, wahoo, tuna, snapper, jacks, and an occasional billlfish.
Freshwater: peacock bass, largemouth and smallmouth bass. There are also bluegill, catfish, and a few species of cichlids.

Time to Go

From April through August is peak season for pelagics. Because of the tropical climate, fishing is great all year.

Top Bait and Lures

- Opelu (scad mackerel) live, dead, or frozen. Squid, mole crabs, and octopus
- Yo-Zuri Crystal Minnows (black and silver)
- 3- to 5-inch paddle tail minnows (white, silver mullet, and super ayu)
- Rapala® Skitter walk (black/silver, chartreuse, and pink)
- Rapala® X-rap (black/silver)

Top Flies

- Crazy charlies size 2-1/0 (tan, pink, orange)
- Gotchas, size 2-1/0 (tan, pink, orange)
- Crab patterns size 2-1/0 (light natural colors)
- Clousers size 1-2/0 (tan, white, chartreuse, and black)
- Small streamers and poppers size 2-2/0 (white, red, and black)

Top Guides

Isaac Brumaghim and Craig Colburn of Aquahunters.

Fish like this great trevally are bruisers to boat fishermen; it is quite a feat to land one from a kayak. Photo by Mike Ichiyama.

Getting to Oahu

Get on a plane and fly to Honolulu, Hawaii. Take the Kamehameha Highway (Highway 83—also known as 80 and 99) around the entire island. Let's face it, there are too many good kayak fishing locations here to list. Rent a kayak, hire a guide, and you will not regret it.

To get to Lake Wilson go to the Wahiawa Freshwater State Recreation Area, located on 380 Walker Avenue in Wahiawa.

- GPS:
  Wahiawa Freshwater State Recreation Area (Lake Wilson)
  21°29'27.56" N, 158°01'35.88" W

Tips

Bring along a big spinner spooled with spectra line, sunscreen, and don't forget to smile—you are in Hawaii! Take advantage of local knowledge, especially the guides. Learn the basics and use this knowledge for future trips.

Difficulty

There is a range of fisheries from mild to wild. I personally cannot rate this place but it is less difficult if you use an experienced guide.

Locally known as "Rocket," Issac Brumaghim poses with a nice gaffer Mahi Mahi. Photo by Ed Evans.

Dragon Run

Middle Peninsula, Virginia

General Info

Dragon Run is one of Virginia's most pristine bodies of water. The Dragon consists of 35 odd miles of swamp that make up the headwaters of the Piankatank River. It has little shoreline development and thus does not suffer the effects of erosion or runoff. It flows through Essex, King and Queen, Middlesex, and Gloucester counties. It is brackish, but has excellent water quality and therefore is an excellent fishery. If you want to see what Virginia rivers looked like before the English settled, then you should think about visiting the Dragon Run.

Fish Species

Popular species include: largemouth bass, bream, catfish, chain pickerel, warmouth, American shad, hickory shad, alewife, blueback herring, and striped bass. As you get farther down river, the salinity increases. There you can expect striped bass, spotted trout, puppy drum, bluefish, and croaker.

Time to Go

Spring and fall are the better months. Hotter weather brings out the biting flies.

Top Lures

- Spinner and buzz baits
- Jerk Shads
- Topwater popping and walk the dog lures
- Small Jigs

Dragon Run is one of the most pristine tidal rivers in Virginia. Photo by Chris Newsome.

Top Flies

- Poppers
- Muddlers
- Hoppers
- Clousers
- Shad Flies

Top Guides

Ruthless Fishing Inc.

Tips

Get help from someone who is familiar with Dragon Run by contacting Friends of Dragon Run at www.dragonrun.org.

Difficulty

The access to Dragon Run is sparse, and I highly suggest using a guide. I give the Dragon a difficulty of 5 on a scale of 1 to 10, but worth the effort.

Getting to Dragon Run

The Dragon has very limited access. The best way to access Dragon Run is by using the area owned and managed by Friends of Dragon Run. This area is located on the Middlesex County side of the Route 603 (Dragon Run Road) bridge. If you are not adventurous, you can fish the area adjacent to the bridge. For targeting saltwater species there is also a public boat ramp off of VA 606 at Freeport in Northwestern Gloucester County. For more information see www.dragonrun.org

- GPS:
  Friends of Dragon Run area:
  37°38'02.03" N, 76°41'43.11" W
  Freeport Boat Ramp:
  37°32'09.57" N, 76°29'44.40" W

To fish the Dragon you need to have at least a full day, but it is worth every second. Photo by Chris Newsome.

Team TKAA's kayaks in the Guana River, just south of Jacksonville, Florida.

Resources

Bow fisherman Tim Chrisman paddles in the shadow of the lodge at Lake Mattamuskeet.

Kayak Fishing Tournaments

The TKAA compound at the 2005 Jamaica Bay Kayak Fish 4 Conservation Tournament. Camping can be a cheap and convenient accommodation for traveling tournament anglers.

Probably the best place to meet other kayak anglers is to participate in a large kayak fishing tournament. I have been competing since 2003 and have learned much by speaking to other kayak anglers. The kayak fishing crowd doesn't hoard information and is always willing to steer fellow kayak anglers in the right direction. Just about all the kayak anglers I know I've met at tournaments. There are several kayak fishing tournaments out there, here are some of the longest running.

Georgia Kayak Fishing Tournament Trail

This three stop tournament series covers the best of Georgia fresh and saltwater fishing.

Time: Spring, Summer, and Fall

Place: Lake Blackshear, Lake Lanier, and Skidaway Narrows

Format: Catch, Photo, and Release

Target Species: Freshwater species include largemouth bass, shoal bass, spotted bass, striped bass, and channel catfish. Saltwater species are spotted trout, redfish and flounder.

Info: www.georgiakayakfishing.com/trail

Jacksonville Kayak Fishing Classic

This charity tournament is the largest of its kind. More than 300 anglers participate in this annual event. The big draws are great divisional prizes and a raffle that includes more than $60,000 in kayak fishing goodies.

Time: Early May

Place: Jacksonville, FL

Format: Catch, Photo, and Release. There are individual species and slam divisions and a fly fishing division. Artificials and bait are allowed.

Target Species: red drum, spotted trout, and flounder

Info: www.jaxkayakfishing.com

Jamaica Bay Kayak Fishing Tournament

This event is held in the shadows of New York City and attracts hundreds of kayak anglers from the Mid-Atlantic and the northeast. Despite its urban setting, Jamaica Bay is a great kayak fishery.

Time: Early May

Place: Brooklyn, New York

Format: Catch, Photo, and Release. Individual species and slam divisions.

Target Species: striped bass, bluefish, and weakfish

Info: www.kayakfish4conservation.com

Competition anglers prepare for a shotgun start on Jamaica Bay.

Mobile Bay Kayak Fishing Association Bagwell Spring Tournament

One of Alabama's largest kayak fishing tournaments.

Time: Mid May

Location: Dauphin Island, AL

Format: Weigh in

Target Species: red drum, spotted trout, and flounder

Info: www.mbkfa.com

New England Kayak Fishing's Mass Bay Striper Shootout

Great single species tournament put on by a great group of kayak anglers.

Time: Late August

Location: Salem, MA

Format: Catch, Photo, and Release

Target Species: striped bass

Info: www.newenglandkayakfishing.com

Most kayak fishing tournaments follow the Catch, Photo, and Release format. This is a picture of a flounder from the Jacksonville Kayak Fishing Classic tournament. With more than 300 anglers, it is the biggest of all kayak fishing tournaments.

Robin Woods measures a redfish for the Tidewater Kayak Anglers Association's annual charity tournament. In 2007, this event attracted 100 competitors from 11 states.

Northern Cal Kayak Anglers' Lake Mendocino Striped Bass Derby

Time: Early October

Location: Lake Mendocino, California

Format: Weigh in

Target Species: striped bass

Info: www.norcalkayakanglers.com

Southwest Florida Council, Boy Scouts of America Kayak Fishing Classic

South Florida tournament that has both youth and adult divisions, great fun for all ages.

Time: Mid May

Place: Fort Meyers, FL

Format: Catch, Photo, and Release

Target Species: snook, snapper, redfish and spotted trout

Info: www.kayakfishingclassic.com

Tidewater Kayak Anglers Association Kayak Fish for Charity Tournament

As the original organizer for this event, it has a special place in my heart. This tournament attracts more than 100 participants and is the largest kayak fishing tournament in the Mid-Atlantic. There are great divisional prizes and more than $20,000 in raffle giveaways.

Time: Late September

Place: Virginia Beach, VA

Format: Catch, Photo, and Release. Individual species and slam divisions.

Target Species: red drum, spotted trout, flounder, and striped bass

Info: www.tkaa.org

Organizing a Tournament

I have spent the last five years organizing and running tournaments. This is one of the best ways to get a group of kayak anglers together. Before you plan a tournament, assign a tournament director who will lead the way through the entire process. Get a volunteer committee organized to help out. The more the merrier! The following checklist is for those who want to run a tournament. No matter how big or small, these guidelines should work.

1. **Time:** Pick a time when the fishery is at its peak. For TKAA, we choose September because it is when participants have the best shot at catching a variety of species.
2. **Location:** Pick an area that has good access and a good fishery. Most tournaments limit their fishing to a designated area or range. We limit our area to within 50 miles of tournament headquarters. You must also find a location to hold your captains' meeting and weigh in. You need to be sure there is ample space for vehicles with kayaks and gear.
3. **Liability:** This is a sticky subject. Most tournaments use signed liability waivers or "hold harmless" forms to protect their organization.

4. **Format:** You must decide what format you want to use. It is up to you to decide whether it is Catch, Photo, and Release (CPR), Catch, Weigh, and Release (CWR), or a kill tournament. Keep in mind that most sponsors prefer the CPR or CWR tournaments. The most successful tournaments are non-profit events. Sponsors like charity events.

5. **Rules:** Once you decide the format, set the rules. These may vary, but the key is to stick with them. Be as specific as possible to avoid any confusion. Stress the use of safety gear, especially the PFD. We disqualify anyone not wearing their PFD at our events.

6. **Sponsors:** When everything is set, start soliciting sponsors for product or money prizes. Be sure to contact them early enough to allow them time to get approval and product. We try to have all our commitments set six months ahead of the tournament.

7. **Promotion:** When you have prizes to give away, start promoting the event. Whether using print, television, or Internet the more promotion the better. We start promoting our event at least nine months in advance.

8. **Volunteers:** Get lots of help. From the initial phase to tournament days, putting together a volunteer committee can make things easy.

9. Have fun and enjoy the tournament!

Chad Hoover with his tournament winning striped bass. Chad won Kayak Fishing Stuff's Jamaica Bay Tournament in New York with this beauty. Photo by Marty Mood.

Kayak Fishing Organizations

Alabama

Mobile Bay Kayak Fishing Association
www.mbkfa.com

Gulf Coast Kayak Fishing Association
www.gulfcoastkayakfishing.com

California

Northern California Kayak Anglers
www.norcalkayakanglers.com

Kayak Fishing Association of California
www.fishingkayaks.net

Florida

Panama City Kayak Fishing
www.pckf.net

Fort Lauderdale Yakfishing Club
www.ftlauderdaleyakfishingclub.org

Paradise Coast Paddlers Club
www.paradisecoastpaddlers.com

Central Florida Kayak Fishing Club
http://groups.yahoo.com/group/OrlandoKayakFishing/

Georgia

Georgia Kayak Fishing
www.georgiakayakfishing.com

Hawaii

Hui Wa'a Kaukahi Kayak Club
www.huiwaa.org

Indiana

Indy-Yaks Kayak Fishing Association
www.indyyaks.com

Louisiana

Bayou Coast Kayak Fishing Club
www.bckfc.org

Young anglers pick up kayak fishing very quickly.

New Jersey

Delaware Valley Kayak Fishing Club
www.delawarevalleykayakandcanoefishingclub.com

New York

Kayak Fishing Association of New York
www.KFA-NY.org

North Carolina

Kayak Fish North Carolina
http://groups.yahoo.com/group/KFNC/

Texas

Paddling Anglers in Canoes and Kayaks (PACK)
www.packtx.org

Virginia

Tidewater Kayak Anglers Association
www.tkaa.org

Williamsburg Kayak Fishing Association
www.wkfa.org

Northern Neck Kayak Anglers Association
www.northernneckforums.com

Kayak Manufacturers

Advanced Elements, Inc.
P.O. Box 5128
Concord, CA 94524
866-262-9076
www.advancedelements.com

Confluence Watersports
Wilderness Systems and Perception
101 Kayaker Way
Easley, SC 29642
864-859-7518
www.confluencewatersports.com
www.wildernesssystems.com
www.perception.com

Emotion Kayaks, Inc.
PO Box 5887
Wyomissing, PA 19610
866-352-9257
www.emotionkayaks.com

Feelfree Kayaks
2004 Riverside Dr., Unit J
Asheville NC 28804
828-254-1101
www.feelfreekayakusa.com

Freedom Hawk Kayaks Inc.
1175 Rickett Rd., Suite 1
Brighton, MI 48116
810-299-2768
www.freedomhawkkayaks.com

Heritage Kayaks
6012 High Point Road
Greensboro, NC 27407
www.heritagekayaks.com

Hobie
4925 Oceanside Blvd.
Oceanside, CA 92056
800-HOBIE-49
www.hobiecat.com

Hurricane Aquasports
170 Water Tank Rd
Warsaw, NC 28398-7821
910-293-2941
www.hurricaneaquasports.com

Kaskazi Kayaks
P.O. Box 50238, Waterfront, 8002
Cape Town, South Africa
+27 (0) 21 439 1134
www.kaskazi.co.za

Malibu Kayaks
7110 Jackson St.
Paramount, CA 90723
877-9-KAYAKS
www.malibukayaks.com

Native Watercraft
6012 High Point Road
Greensboro, NC 27407
www.nativewatercraft.net

NuCanoe Inc.
PO Box 28636
Bellingham, WA 98228
888-226-6310
www.nucanoe.com

Ocean Kayak, Necky, and Old Towne Canoes
2460 Salashan Loop
P.O. Box 5003
Ferndale, Washington 98248-5003
800-8-KAYAKS
www.oceankayak.com

Pelican International Inc.
1000, Place Paul-Kane
Laval Qc Canada
H7C 2T2
888-669-6960
www.pelicansport.com

Kayak Accessory Manufacturers

Electronics

Eagle Electronics
P.O. Box 669
Catoosa, OK 74015-0669
800-324-1354
www.eaglenav.com

Garmin
1200 E. 151st Street
Olathe, KS 66062-3426
913-397-8200
www.garmin.com

Humminbird
678 Humminbird Lane
Eufaula, AL 36027
800-633-1468
www.humminbird.com

Lowrance
12000 E. Skelly Drive
Tulsa, OK 74128
800-324-1356
www.lowrance.com

Paddles

Adventure Technology
1308 Industrial Road
Hood River, OR 97031
877-766-4757
www.atpaddle.com

Aqua-Bound Technology Ltd
PMB #159-1160 Yew Avenue
Blaine, WA 98230
602-882-2052
www.aquabound.com

Bending Branches
812 Prospect Court
Osceola, WI 54020
866-755-3405
www.bendingbranches.com

Canon Paddles
P.O. Box 19346
Minneapolis, MN 55419-0346
800-758-1720
www.cannonpaddles.com

Jimbo Meador with a Nova Scotia salmon. Photo courtesy of Jimbo Meador.

Chad Hoover fighting a nice Florida redfish.

Carlisle and Lendal Paddles
P.O. Box 548
35 Middle Street
Old Town, ME 04468
800-343-1555
www.carlislepaddles.com
www.lendal.com

Water Trail Gear
6012 High Point Road
Greensboro, NC 27407
www.watertrailgear.com

Werner Paddles, Inc.
33415 SR 2
Sultan, WA 98294
800-275-3311
www.wernerpaddles.com

PFDs, Paddle Wear, and Safety Equipment

Astral Buoyancy Company
2002 Riverside Drive
Dock 42A
Asheville, NC 28804
828-255-2638
www.astralbuoyancy.com

Extrasport Inc.
2460 Salashan Loop
Ferndale, WA 98248
800-852-9257
www.extrasport.com

Kokatat
5350 Ericson Way
Arcata, CA 95521
800.225.9749
www.kokatat.com

Lateral Line, Inc.
620 South Street
Easton, MD 21601
443-569-3701
www.laterallineco.com

MTI Adventurewear LLC
P.O. Box 210
Plympton, MA 02367
800-783-4684
www.mtiadventurewear.com

NRS Northwest River Supply
2009 S. Main Street
Moscow, ID 83843
877-677-4327
www.nrsweb.com

Kayak Fishing Guides

ALASKA

Ketchikan Kayak Fishing
P.O. Box 5011
Ketchikan, Alaska 99901
Contact: Howard McKim
907-225-1272
trips@yakfishalaska.com
www.yakfishalaska.com

BAJA, MEXICO

Gary Bulla's Fishing Adventures
Baja, Mexico
Contact: Gary Bulla
805-933-1367
info@garybulla.com
www.garybulla.com

BELIZE

Slickrock Adventures
P.O. Box 1400
Moab, UT 84532
800-390-5715 (toll free)
slickrock@slickrock.com
www.slickrock.com

CALIFORNIA

Bowman Bluewater Guides & Outfitters, LLC
P.O. Box 975
Cardiff, CA 92007
Contact: Conway Bowman
619-822-6256
conwaybowman@gmail.com
www.bowmanbluewater.com

Kayak Fishing.com
Los Angeles/Malibu/East Cape, Mexico
Contact: Dennis Spike and Jeff Kriger
818-970-2392
spike@kayakfishing.com
www.kayakfishing.com

La Jolla Kayak Fishing Adventures
La Jolla, CA
Contact: Jim Sammons
619-461-7172
www.lajollakayakfishingadventures.com
Jim@Kayak4Fish.com

Sunrise on the York River in Gloucester Point, Virginia.

COLORADO

Dvorak Expeditions
Gunnison River, Colorado
Contact: Jaci Dvorak
800-824-3795
info@dvorakexpeditions.com
www.dvorakexpeditions.com

CONNECTICUT

Yakdawgs Guide Service
Central and Eastern Connecticut
Contact: Kevin Mucha and Roland St. Denis
860-798-5218
rol@yakdawgs.com
www.yakdawgs.com

FLORIDA

Adventure Kayak Fishing
Palm Harbor, FL
Contact: Neil Taylor
727-692-6345
LivelyBaits@aol.com
www.adventurekayakfishing.com

Complete Fly-Fishing Schools and Expeditions
2280 Packard Avenue
Oviedo, FL 32765
Contact: Jon B. Cave
407-977-0659
jon@joncaveflyfishing.com
www.joncaveflyfishing.com

Everglades Kayak Fishing
P.O. Box 670
Everglades City, FL 34139
Contact: Captain Charles Wright
239-695-9107
Captwright@ChokoloskeeCharters.com
www.EvergladesKayakFishing.com

Florida Kayak Fishing
3323 SE 2nd Street
Ocala, FL 34471
Contact: Captain Ken Daubert
352-624-1878
kendaubert@floridakayakfishing.com
www.floridakayakfishing.com

Grande Tours, Inc.
12575 Placida Road
Placida, FL 33946
Contact: Captain Marian Schneider and Dave Loger
941-697-8825
captmarian@grandetours.com
dave@adventurekayakfishing.com
www.grandetours.com

High Tailin Charters Inc.
Fort Myers, FL
Contact: David McCleaf and Shane Edgar
239-994-4925
239-770-4614
wadefisher616@yahoo.com
smedgar@eagle.fgcu.edu
www.hightailincharters.com

Kayak Mike's Charters
Jacksonville, FL
Contact: Captain Mike Kogan
904-382-5007
info@kayakmike.com
www.kayakmike.com

Mosquito Coast Fishing Charters
540 Lake Lenelle Drive
Chuluota, FL 32766
Contact: Captain Tom Van Horn
407-366-8085 (landline)
407-416-1187 (on the water)
866-790-8081 (toll free)
captain@irl-fishing.com
www.irl-fishing.com

Oasis Angling Adventures, Inc.
Doral, FL
Contact: Jim Dussias
305-766-2926
jdussia1@earthlink.net

Peter Hinck (Heritage Endorsed Guide)
230 Ponce de Leon Street
Royal Palm Beach, FL 33411
Contact: Peter Hinck
561-951-2667
palmbeachpete@yahoo.com

Southern Drawl Kayak Fishing
2519 Wood Oak Drive
Sarasota, FL 34232
Contact: Steve Gibson
941-284-3406
steve@kayakfishingsarasota.com
www.kayakfishingsarasota.com

Steinhatchee Kayak Tours, LLC
Steinhatchee, FL
Contact: Mark Fisher
352-213-7057
SteinhatcheeKayakTours@yahoo.com
www.steinhatcheekayaktours.com

HAWAII

Aquahunters
Oahu, Hawaii
Contact: Isaac Brumaghim and Craig Colburn
808-779-1472
isaac@aquahunters.com
www.aquahunters.com

LOUISIANA

Calmwater Charters
P.O. Box 657
275 Rosethorne
Grand Isle, LA 70358
Contact: Captain Danny Wray
225-721-8182
calmwater@myviscom.com
www.calmwatercharters.net

Go For IT! Charters
43207 Hwy 190 E
Slidell, LA 70461
Contact: Captain Gary Taylor
985-641-8532
fishinla@bellsouth.net
www.goforitcharters.com

MASSACHUSETTS

Cape Cod Fishing Guides
375 Great Western Road
Harwich, MA 02645
Contact: Michael Mullaney
508-208-2265
Mully8@msn.com
www.capecodfishingguide.com

Northeast Kayak and Boat Charters
Springfield, MA
Contact: Captain Jerry Sparks
413-219-8455
jsparks132@yahoo.com
www.sparkskayakfish.com

MICHIGAN

Golden Drake Outdoors
9280 McGregor Road
Pinckney, MI 48169
Contact: Craig Kivi
ckil1046@aol.com
www.goldendrake.com

Uncle Ducky Charters
434 East Ptrospect
Marquette, MI 49855
877-288-5447
info@uncleducky.com
www.uncleducky.com

MISSISSIPPI

Shore Thing Fishing Charters
7816 Hilo Place
Diamondhead, MS 39525
Contact: Captain Mike Thompson, Jr.
228-342-2206
capt_mike@shorethingcharters.com
www.shorethingcharters.com

NEBRASKA

Kayakjak's Kayak Fishing Guide Service
Benkleman, NE
Contact: Marty Hughes
308-423-2478
info@kayakjak.com
www.kayakjak.com

NEW YORK

RiverBay Flyfishing Outfitters
Long Island, NY
Contact: John Fischer
516-425-4198
631-842-2880 (reservations)
john@riverbayflyfishing.com
www.riverbayflyfishing.com

NORTH CAROLINA

Cape Fear Kayaks and Outfitters
435 Eastwood Road
Wilmington, NC 28403
Contact: Chris Tryon
910-547-6989
888-794-4867 (toll free)
ctryon_14@yahoo.com
www.capefearkayaks.com

Get Outdoors
Mebane, NC
Contact: Philip Ruckart
336-324-9405
yak4fish@mac.com
http://web.mac.com/ruckartphoto/iWeb/Yak4fish/Home.html

TEXAS

Blue Heron Adventures
Corpus Christi, TX
Contact: Captain Steve Utley
361-334-2336
steven@blueheronadventures.com
www.blueheronadventures.com

Brew-Skies Shallow Water Adventures
Rockport, TX
Contact: Captain Jason Brou
361-403-7077
icecoldbrew@cableone.net
www.tripleboutdoors.com/brewskieshome.htm

Slowride Guide Services
821 South Commercial
Aransas Pass, TX 78336
Contact: Captain Dean Thomas
866-856-9477 (toll free)
slowrideguide@cableone.net
www.slowrideguide.com

Cameron Washington with his first Lynnhaven Inlet redfish.

Snookdude Kayak Fishing Charters
Houston, TX
Contact: Captain Ruben Garza
832-385-1431
rgjshg@peoplepc.com
www.snookdudekayakfishingcharters.com

VIRGINIA/MARYLAND

Blue Ridge Kayak Fishing
Virginia/Maryland
Contact: Jeff Little
410-635-3957
www.blueridgekayakfishing.com

Ocean Eagle Kayak Adventures
Virginia Beach, VA
Contact: Stephen Zawisa
757-589-1766
stephen@oceaneaglekayak.com
www.oceaneaglekayak.com

Ruthless Fishing Inc.
Virginia Beach, VA
Contact: Cory "Ruthless" Routh and Mark Lozier
757-403-0734
cory@ruthlessfishing.com
www.ruthlessfishing.com

Kayak Web sites

All Kayak Fishing
Great retail Web site with a popular FAQ section
www.allkayakfishing.com

American Canoe Association
Top kayak and canoe safety and instruction organization
www.americancanoe.com

Austin Kayak Fishing
Austin's premier kayak fishing forum
www.austinkayakfishing.com

Bay Tubers
Fishing site for float tubers and kayakers alike
www.baytubers.com

Big Waters Edge
California Web site with lots of info and video
www.bigwatersedge.com

Coastal Kayak Angler
Texas-based kayak fishing forum
www.coastalkayakangler.com

Coastal Kayak Fishing
Original kayak fishing forum that started it all
www.kayakfishing.com

East Coast Kayak Fishing
Informational Web site covers the entire East Coast
www.eastcoastkayakfishing.com

Florida Kayak Fishing
Specialty site for light tackle and fly fishing kayak anglers
www.floridakayakfishing.com

Jacob Hines with trophy redfish caught off of High Island, Texas. The attraction was fresh cut mullet on a weightless rig, and the fish was released unharmed. Photo by Mario Benavides.

Forgotten Coast Kayak Anglers
Florida-based Web site covering the northern Gulf Coast
www.fcka.net

Hook 1 Kayak Fishing Gear
Retail site with great accessories
www.kayakfishinggear.com

Hooked on Kayaks
Retail Web site featuring great kayak fishing accessories
www.hookedonkayaks.com

Jacksonville Kayak Fishing
Kayak fishing forum and home of the largest kayak fishing tournament
www.jaxkayakfishing.com

Kayak Anglers Society of America
Grassroots organization for military and collegiate kayak fishing events
www.kayakanglerssa.org/clubs/

Kayak Fishing Magazine
Monthly online magazine covering kayak fishing
www.kayakfishingmagazine.net

Kayak Fishing Records
Web site listing the biggest fish caught from a kayak
www.kayakfishingrecords.com

Kayak Fishing Stuff
Retail Web site with informative forums
www.kayakfishingstuff.com

Kayak Sportfishing
One of the longest running kayak fishing Web sites
www.kayaksportfishing.com

La Jolla Kayak Fishing Adventures
San Diego's original kayak fishing Web site
www.Kayak4Fish.com

Michigan Kayak Fishing
Informational Web site by well-traveled kayak anglers
www.michigankayakfishing.com

Northwest Kayak Anglers
Kayak fishing in the Pacific Northwest
www.northwestkayakanglers.com

Paddle Fishing
Florida-based kayak fishing forum
www.paddle-fishing.com

Paddling.net
General paddling Web site with great articles about kayak fishing
www.paddling.net

Plastic Navy
Kayak fishing forums covering all of Southern California
www.plasticnavy.com

Ruthless Fishing
Official Web site of *Kayak Fishing: The Complete Guide*
www.ruthlessfishing.com

Sit On Top Kayaking
Site dedicated to general sit-on-top kayaking
www.sit-on-topkayaking.com

Space Coast Kayak Fishing
Blog discussing kayak fishing in central Florida
http://spacecoastkayakfishing.blogspot.com/

Texas Kayak Fisherman
Texas' largest kayak fishing forum
www.texaskayakfisherman.com

Ultimate Kayak Fishing
Connecticut-based information Web site
www.ultimatekayakfishing.com

Yak Dawgs Kayak Fishing
Northeast-based kayak fishing Web site
www.yakdawgs.com

Yak Fishing
California forum dedicated to kayak fishing
www.yakfishing.com

Mark Lozier gets a good start on a wonderful day of kayak fishing.

Conservation

No Nonsense Fly Fishing Guidebooks believes that, in addition to local information and gear, fishers need clean water and healthy fish. We encourage preservation, improvement, conservation, enjoyment and understanding of our waters and their inhabitants. While fishing, take care of the place, practice catch and release and try to avoid spawning fish.

When you aren't fishing, a good way to help all things wild and aquatic is to support organizations dedicated to these ideas. We encourage you to get involved, learn more and to join such organizations.

American Rivers........(202) 347-7550
Blackfoot Challenge........(406) 793-9300
California Trout........(415) 392-8887
Chesapeake Bay Foundation—VA Chapter........(804) 780-1392
Coastal Conservation Association Virginia........(804) 347-7858
Deschutes Basin Land Trust........(541) 330-0017
Federation of Fly Fishers........(406) 585-7592
International Game Fish Association........(954) 927-2628
International Women Fly Fishers........(925) 934-2461
New Mexico Trout........(505) 884-5262
Oregon Trout........(503) 222-9091
Outdoor Writers Association of America........(406) 728-7434
Recreational Fishing Alliance........(888) JOIN-RFA
Rails-to-Trails Conservancy........(202) 331-9696
Sierra Club........(415) 977-5500
Theodore Roosevelt Conservation Partnership........(877) 770-8722
Trout Unlimited........(800) 834-2419

Saving a National Treasure

CALIFORNIA TROUT

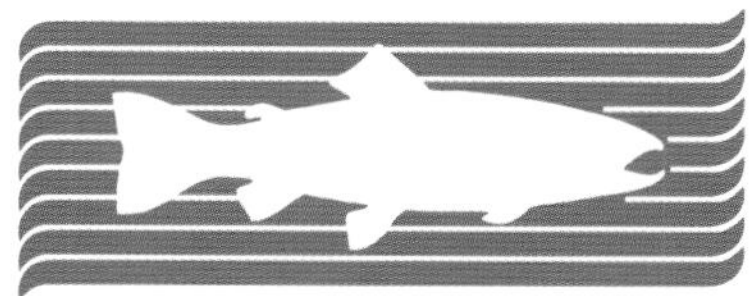

KEEPER OF THE STREAMS

Fly Fishing Knots

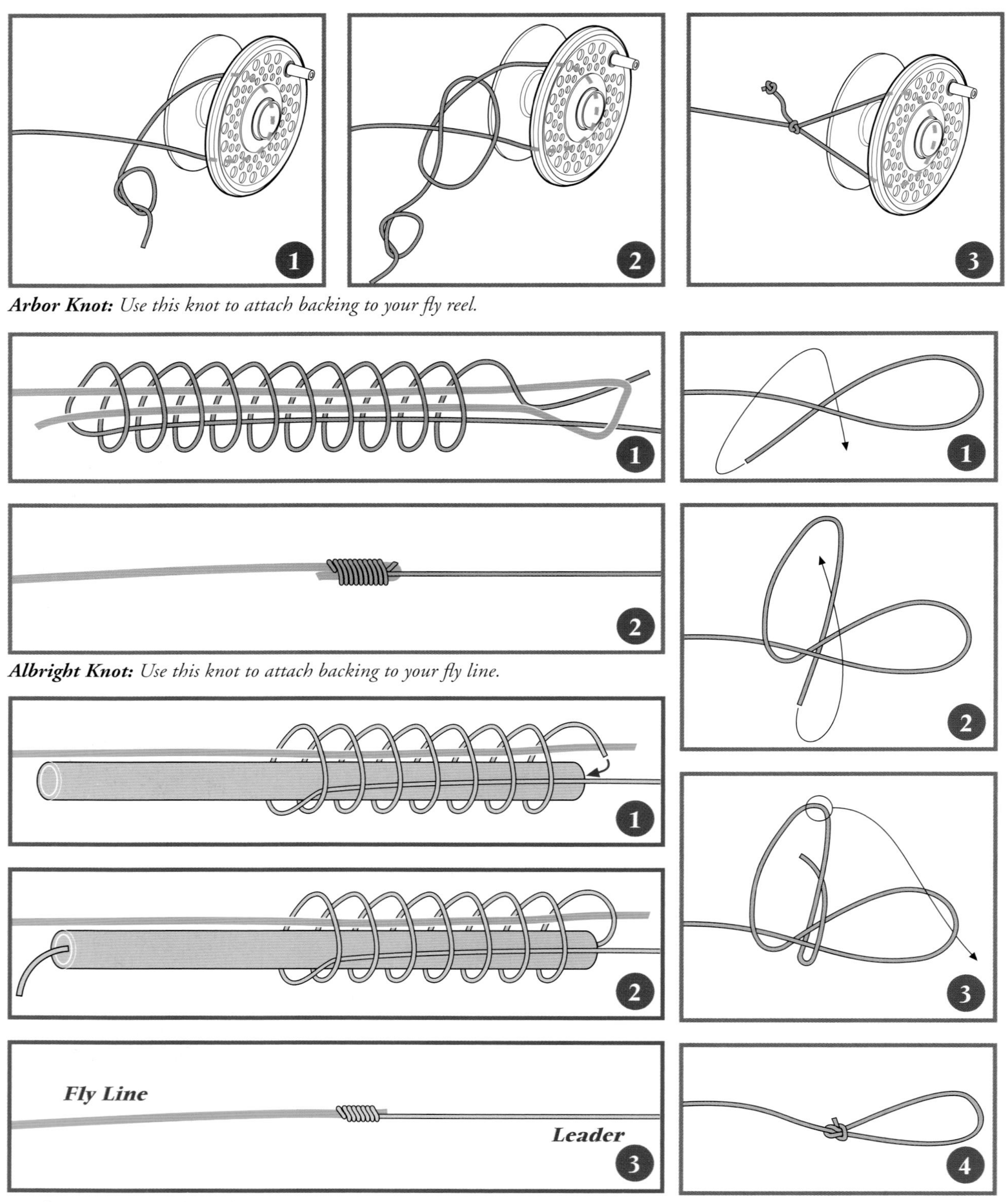

Arbor Knot: *Use this knot to attach backing to your fly reel.*

Albright Knot: *Use this knot to attach backing to your fly line.*

Nail Knot: *Use a nail, needle or a tube to tie this knot, which connects the forward end of the fly line to the butt end of the leader. Follow this with a Perfection Loop and you've got a permanent end loop that allows easy leader changes.*

Perfection Loop: *Use this knot to create a loop in the butt end of the leader for loop-to-loop connections.*

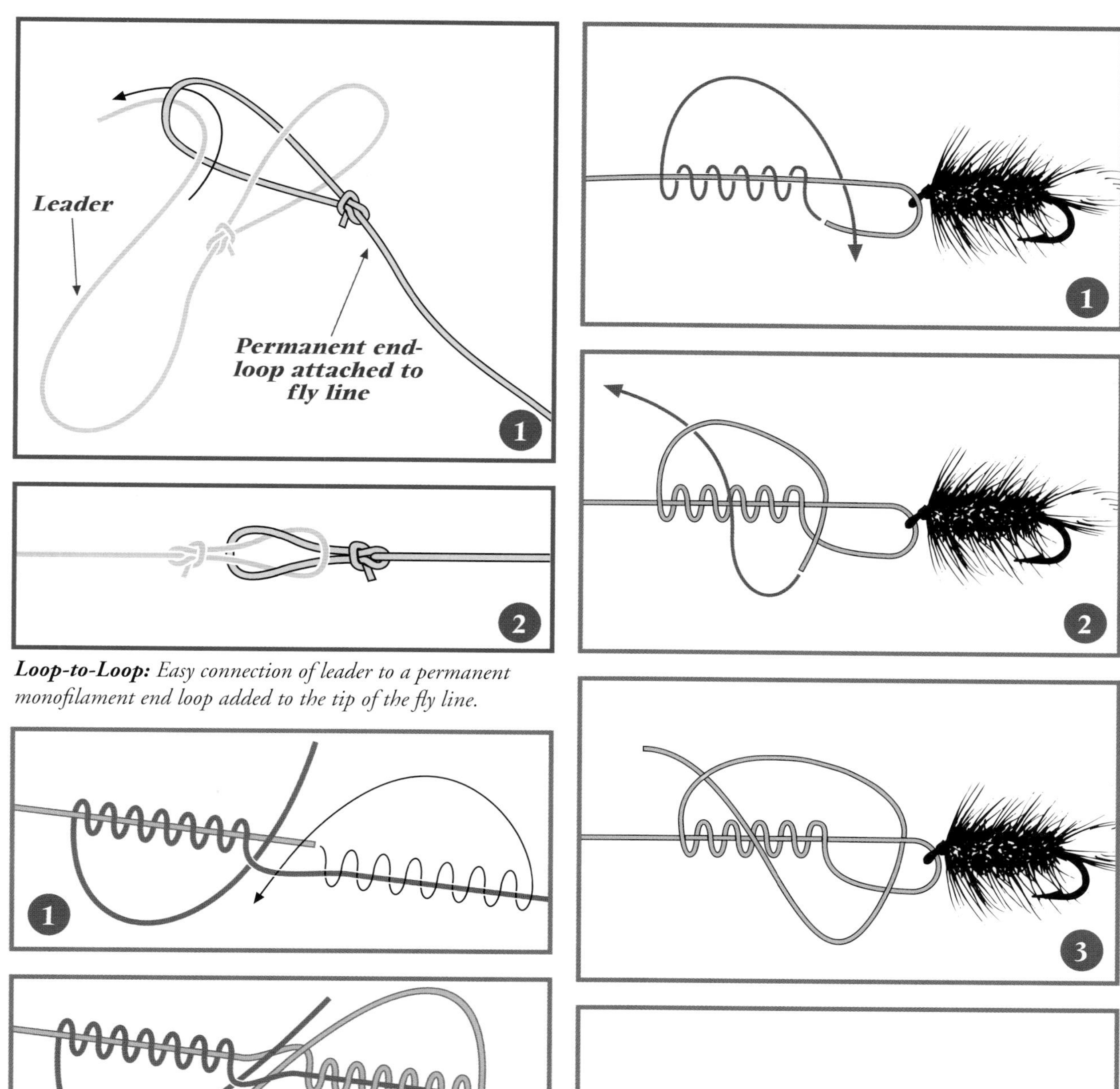

Loop-to-Loop: *Easy connection of leader to a permanent monofilament end loop added to the tip of the fly line.*

Blood Knot: *Use this knot to connect sections of leader tippet material. Hard to tie, but worth the effort.*

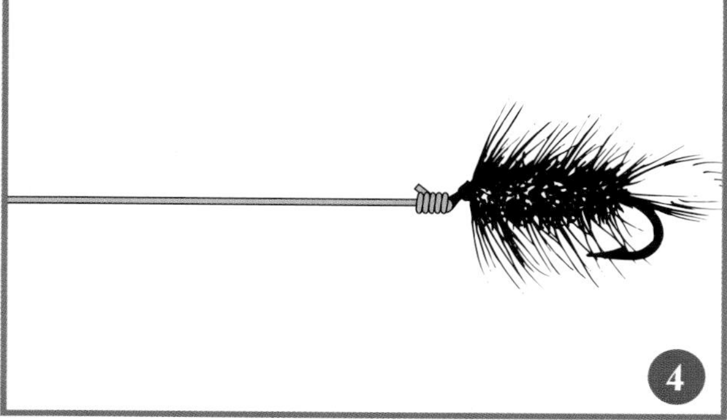

Improved Clinch Knot: *Use this knot to attach the fly to the end of the tippet. Remember to moisten the knot before pulling it up tight.*

General Fishing Knots and Rigs

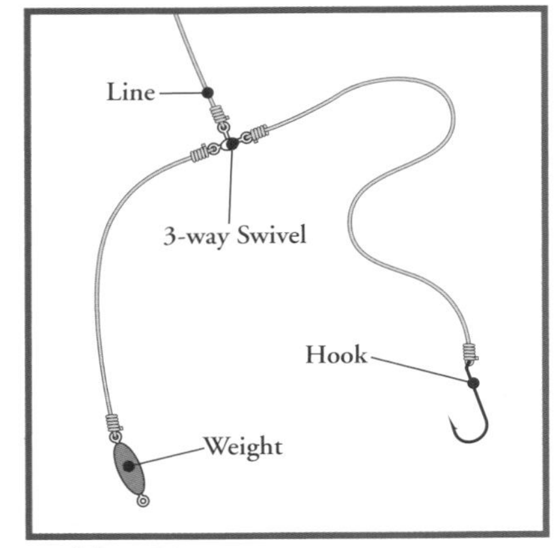

Halibut Rig

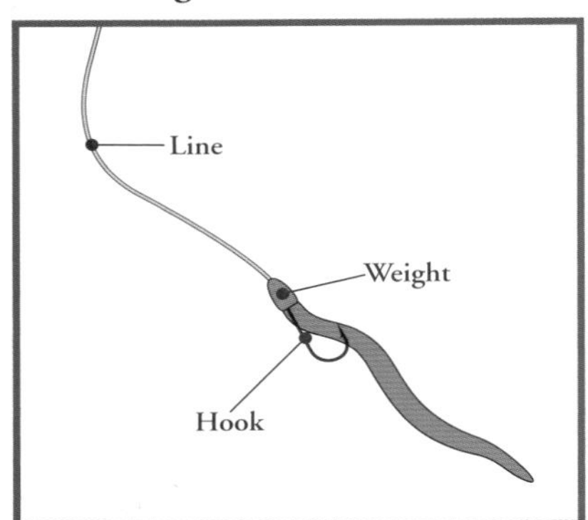

Texas Rig

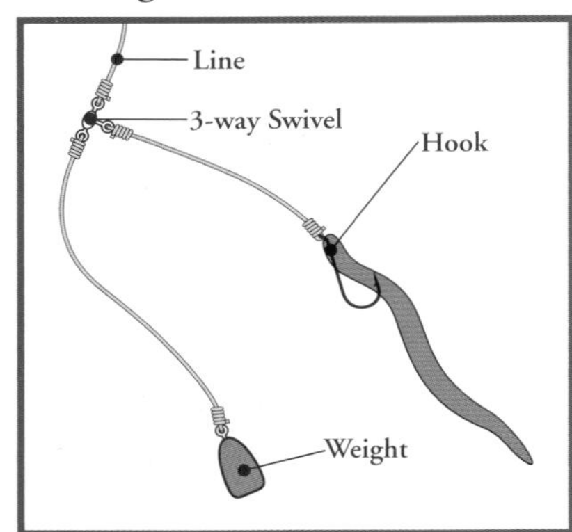

Drop-shot Rig

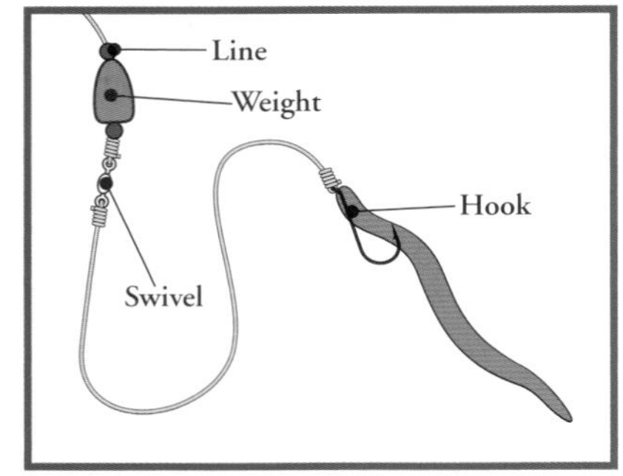

Carolina Rig

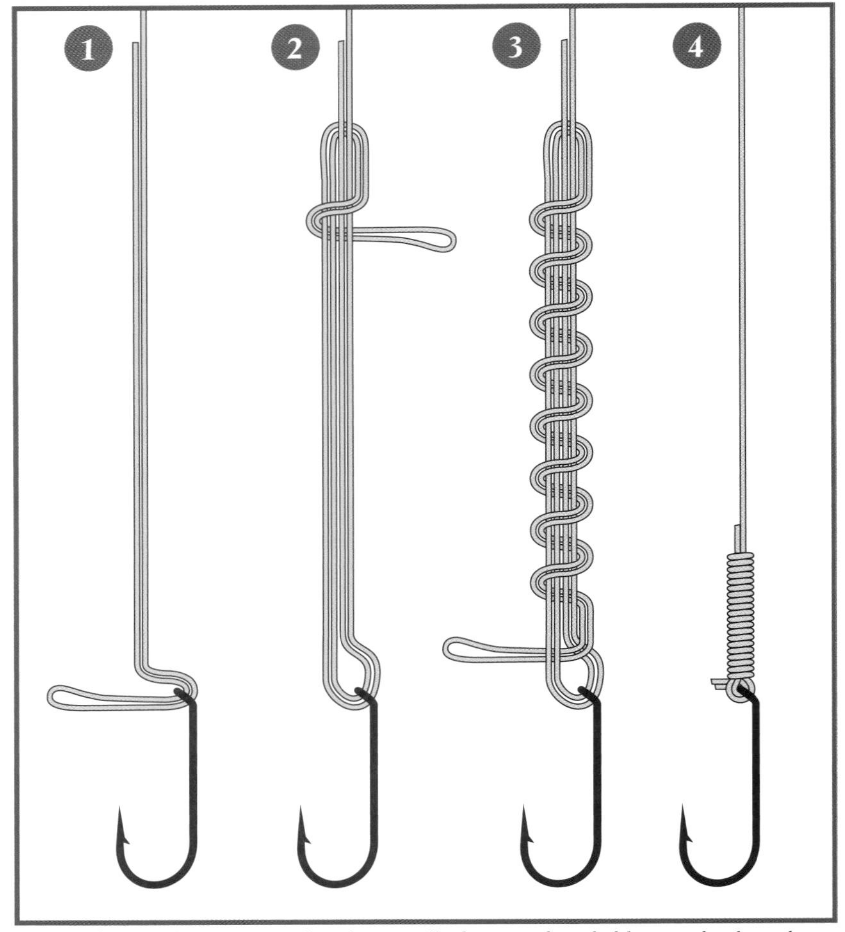

Berkley® Braid Knot: *Developed especially for tying braided lines to hooks or lures.*

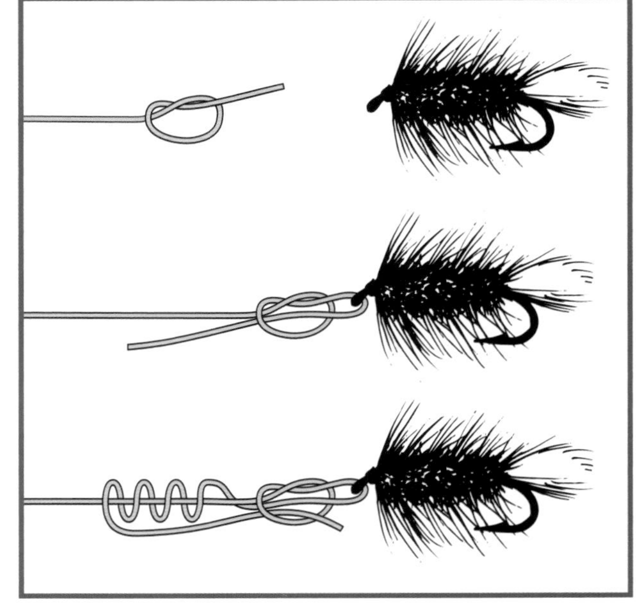

Non-slip Loop Knot

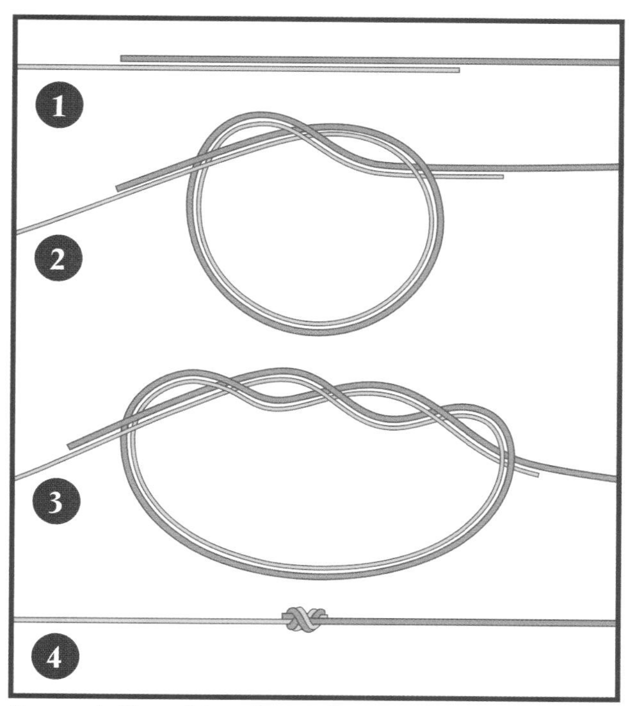

Surgeon's Knot: *Most often used in tying leaders to line, especially when diameters are different.*

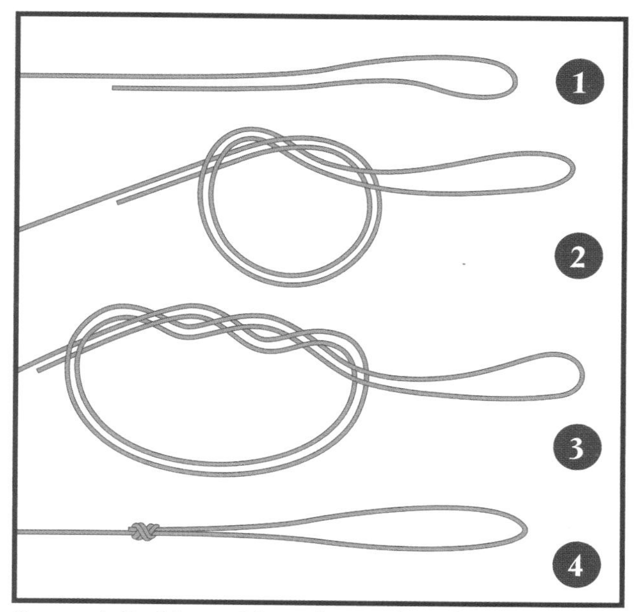

Surgeon's End Loop: *Place a loop at the end of the line and tie just like the surgeon's knot to provide a loop at the end of the line or leader.*

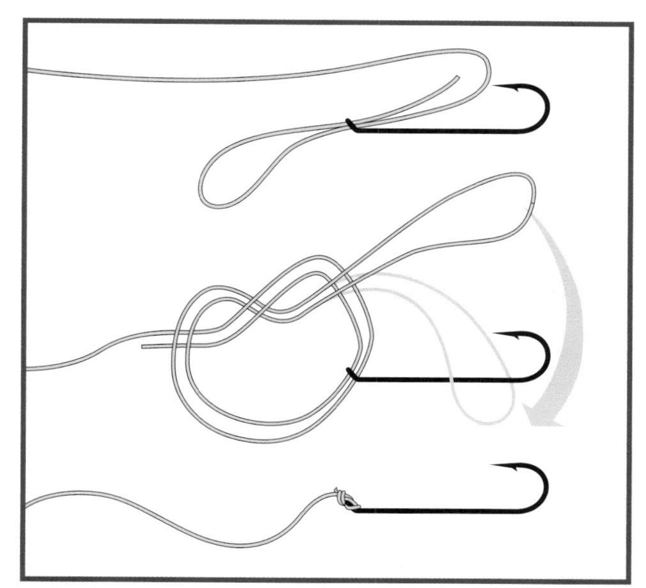

Palomar Knot: *A very strong knot to attach lures, hooks, or swivels.*

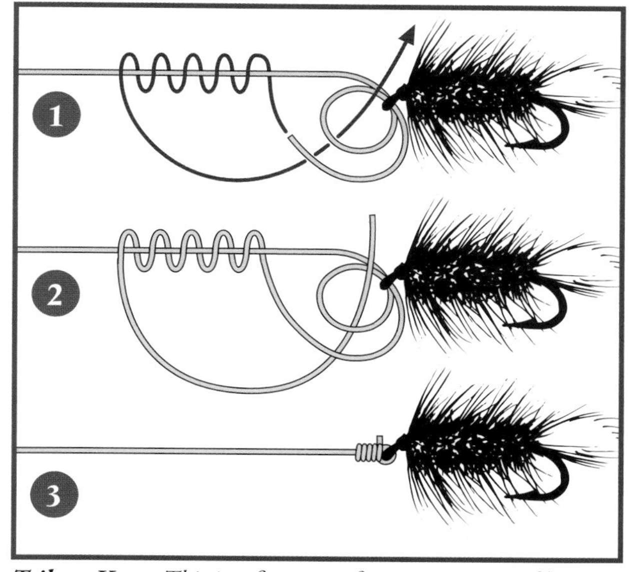

Trilene Knot: *This is a fine way of connecting monofilament line to lures, hooks, or swivels.*

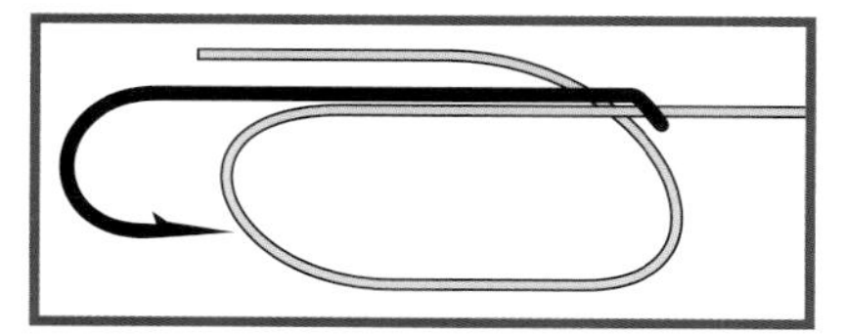

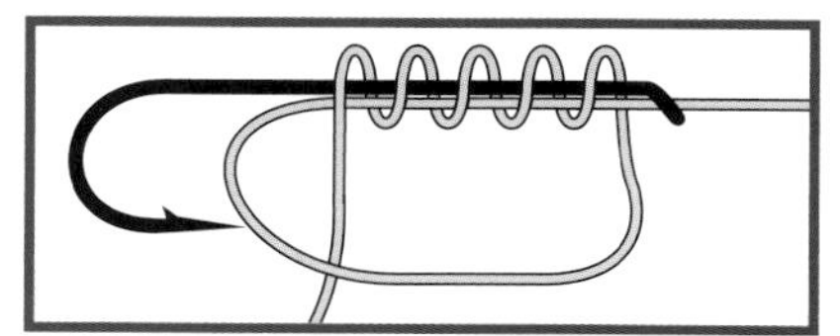

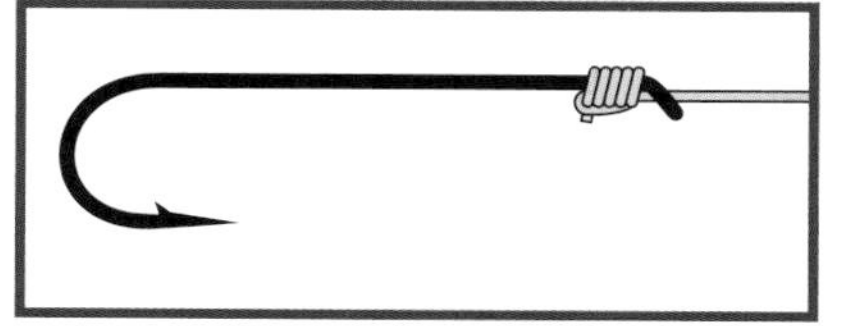

Snell Knot: *A great way to attach a bait hook to the end of the line. There are many differing instructions on how to tie a snell knot.*

Find Your Way with These No Nonsense Guides

Fly Fishing Arizona
Glenn Tinnin

Desert, forest, lava fields, red rocks and canyons. Here is where to go and how to fish 32 cold water and warm water streams, lakes, and reservoirs in Arizona. Newly revised.
ISBN-10 1-892469-02-2 .... $19.95
ISBN-13 978-1-892469-02-1

Fly Fishing Southern Baja
Gary Graham

With this book you can fly to Baja, rent a car and go out on your own to find exciting saltwater fly fishing! Mexico's Baja Peninsula is now one of the premier destinations for saltwater fly anglers.
ISBN-10 1-892469-00-6 .... $18.95
ISBN-13 978-1-892469-00-7

Fly Fishing California
Ken Hanley

Ken Hanley's vast experience fly fishing in California gives you a clear understanding of the best places to fish across the state of California—from the Baja coast to the northern wilderness.
ISBN-10 1-892469-10-3 $28.95
ISBN-13 978-1-892469-10-6

Fishing Central California
Brian Milne

This comprehensive and entertaining guide will improve your chances every time you cast a line in Central California and beyond. You'll learn where the best spots are on the small streams, rivers, lakes, and ocean fisheries. How to select the right baits, lures, and equipment. Full color.
ISBN-10 1-892469-18-9.......... $24.95
ISBN-13 978-1-892469-18-2

Fly Fishing Colorado
Jackson Streit

Your experienced guide gives you the quick, clear understanding of the essential information you'll need to fly fish Colorado's most outstanding waters. Use this book to plan your Colorado fly fishing trip, and take this guide along for ready reference. This popular guide has been updated, redesigned and is in its third printing. Full color.
ISBN-10 1-892469-13-8 .... $19.95
ISBN-13 978-1-892469-13-7

Fly Fishing Idaho
Bill Mason

The Henry's Fork, Salmon, Snake and Silver Creek plus 24 other waters. Bill Mason shares his 30 plus years of Idaho fly fishing. Revised.
ISBN-10 1-892469-17-0 .... $18.95
ISBN-13 978-1-892469-17-5

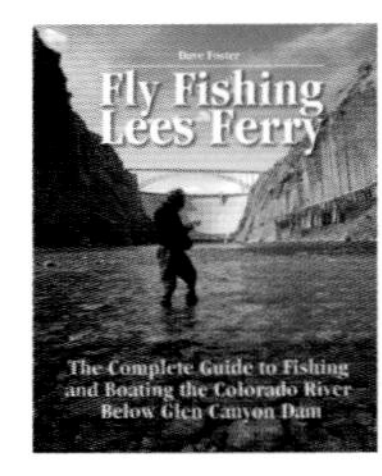

Fly Fishing Lees Ferry
Dave Foster

This guide provides a clear understanding of the complex and fascinating 15 miles of river that can provide fly anglers 40-fish days. Detailed maps direct fly and spin fishing access. Learn about history, boating, and geology. Indispensable for the angler and intrepid visitor to the Marble Canyon. Revised.
ISBN-10 1-892469-15-4 .... $18.95
ISBN-13 978-1-892469-15-1

Fly Fishing Magdalena Bay
Gary Graham

Guide and excursion leader Gary Graham (*Baja On The Fly*) lays out the truth about fly fishing for snook in mangroves, and off-shore marlin. Photos, illustrations, maps, and travel information, this is "the Bible" for this unique region.
ISBN-10 1-892469-08-1 .... $24.95
ISBN-13 978-1-892469-08-3

Seasons of the Metolius
John Judy

This book describes how a beautiful riparian environment both changes and stays the same over the years. Mr. Judy makes his living in nature and chronicles his 30 years of study, writing, and fly fishing his beloved home water, the crystal clear Metolius River in Central Oregon.

ISBN-10 1-892469-11-1 .... $20.95
ISBN-13 978-1-892469-11-3

Fly Fishing Montana
Brian & Jenny Grossenbacher

Explore Montana—a fly angler's Mecca—as Brian and Jenny Grossenbacher guide you through their beautiful home state. You'll get the information you need to fly fish Montana's outstanding waters.

ISBN-10 1-892469-14-6 ...... $28.9 5
ISBN-13 978-1-892469-14-4

Fly Fishing Nevada
Dave Stanley

The Truckee, Walker, Carson, Eagle, Davis, Ruby, mountain lakes and more. Mr. Stanley is recognized nationwide as the most knowledgeable fly fisher and outdoorsman in Nevada. He owns and operates the Reno Fly Shop and Truckee River Outfitters in Truckee, California.

ISBN-10 0-9637256-2-9 .... $18.95
ISBN-13 978-0-9637256-2-2

Fly Fishing New Mexico
Taylor Streit

Since 1970, Mr. Streit has been New Mexico's foremost fly fishing authority and professional guide. He owned the Taos Fly Shop for ten years and managed a bone fishing lodge in the Bahamas. Taylor makes winter fly fishing pilgrimages to Argentina where he escorts fly fishers and explorers. Newly revised.

ISBN-10 1-892469-04-9 .... $19.95
ISBN-13 978-1-892469-04-5

Fly Fishing Central & Southeastern Oregon
Harry Teel

New waters, maps, hatch charts and illustrations. The best fly fishing in this popular region. Full color.

ISBN-10 1-892469-09-X $19.95
ISBN-13 978-1-892469-09-0

Fly Fishing Pyramid Lake
Terry Barron

The Gem of the Desert is full of huge Lahontan Cutthroat trout. Terry has recorded everything you need to fly fish the most outstanding trophy cutthroat fishery in the U.S. Where else can you get tired of catching 18–25" trout?

ISBN-10 0-9637256-3-7 .... $15.95
ISBN-13 978-0-9637256-3-9

Fly Fishing Utah
Steve Schmidt

Utah yields extraordinary, uncrowded and little known fishing. Steve Schmidt, outfitter and owner of Western Rivers Fly Shop in Salt Lake City has explored these waters for over 28 years. Covers mountain streams and lakes, tailwaters, and reservoirs.

ISBN-10 0-9637256-8-8 .... $19.95
ISBN-13 978-0-9637256-8-4

Fly Fishing Virginia
Beau Beasley

From urban streams to the Shenandoah National Park, Beau Beasley shows you where to fly fish in Virginia. Detailed maps, photographs, and Beasley's wisdom guide you through the many waters in the Old Dominion. Full color.

ISBN-10 1-892469-16-2 ...... $28.95
ISBN-13 978-1-892469-16-8

Business Traveler's Guide To Fly Fishing in the Western States
Bob Zeller

A seasoned road warrior reveals where one can fly fish within a two-hour drive of every major airport in thirteen western states.

ISBN-10 1-892469-01-4 .... $18.95
ISBN-13 978-1-892469-01-4

A Woman's Guide To Fly Fishing Favorite Waters
Yvonne Graham

Forty-five of the top women fly fishing experts reveal their favorite waters. From spring creeks in the East, trout waters in the Rockies to exciting Baja: all from the female perspective.

ISBN-10 1-892469-03-0 .... $19.95
ISBN-13 978-1-892469-03-0

Aaron Johnson with his Necky Chatham 17 rigged out for fishing.

Ultimate 14.5 ready for a day on the water in Cherrystone Inlet, Virginia.

Last Cast

I hope you found my book educational and enjoyable. It has been a challenging and fun project. I have a newfound respect for the everyday guy who writes a book and the families who put up with it. This project started out as a few kayak fishing articles and has now materialized into a complete kayak fishing guide. I hope the information has inspired both beginner and experienced kayak anglers. I cannot stress enough that you should use the expertise of retailers, instructors, and guides in your quest to become a kayak angler. As the sport continues to grow, so will the commitment to provide advice on techniques and equipment.

I truly hope you enjoyed the book and are on your way to buy a kayak, get paddling lessons, or book a guide. As for me, it's time to save this document, shut down the computer, and get back to being "Daddy." Thanks again for checking out my book and I'll see you on the water!

There is nothing like kicking up your feet and enjoying the ending of a great day of kayak fishing.